A People's History of
LEICESTER

A Pictorial History of Working Class Life and Politics

Ned Newitt

'Labour is the source of wealth
The profits of the earth are for all'
– a Leicester Chartist slogan from 1838 and
of the Leicester unemployed in 1905

breedon **books**
PUBLISHING

First published in Great Britain in 2008 by
The Breedon Books Publishing Company Limited
Breedon House, 3 The Parker Centre,
Derby, DE21 4SZ.

ISBN 978-1-85983-646-0

Printed and bound in China.

Top: Two women porters at work on the platform of Leicester Central Station, c.1920. Before World War One large numbers of local women went out to work, however, it was unusual for women to work on the railways. The labour shortage caused by the war drew women into new areas of work. The identity of the woman on the left is unknown but the lady on the right has been identified as Lucy Lount.

The leaders of the 1905 Unemployed March in Leicester Market Place, shortly before their departure to London.

Women at work in the Harrison and Hayes hosiery factory, Asylum Street, 1928.

Bottom: a wheel-tapper at work checking the wheels of a bogie carriage at Leicester Central Station, c.1910. The job of a wheel-tapper was to test wheels for cracks or fractures.

Contents

A woman filling a bucket at the rear of Nos 3–15 White Street (off Causeway Lane, leading to Grape Street). There were 10 houses in this yard served by one common tap, two small wash houses (on the left) and four WCs. On the right is the covered entrance between Nos 16 and 17 White Street which led from the front street. In 1935, after receiving a notice to quit from the landlord, the wife of the tenant of No. 17 committed suicide. The tenants of these houses were rehoused on North Braunstone Estate between October 1938 and April 1939 and the houses were demolished in 1939.

Introduction

In 1900 Leicester was a very different city. It was a manufacturing town whose industries were dominated by the hosiery and boot and shoe trade. A huge swathe of slum housing covered an area now occupied by the ring road from St Mark's Church round to the Holiday Inn. It was in these poor districts of two-roomed houses and courtyards that the ravages of poverty, TB, smallpox and infant mortality were felt.

Leicester had a radical tradition stretching back to the Jacobins of the 1790s. The town had been at the centre of agitation for the extension of the franchise through both the reform movement and the People's Charter. There was a strong and diverse tradition of radical thought, whether it came from Owen's ideas on co-operation and socialism, the Chartist agitation against poverty, or from Liberal reformers and trade union pioneers.

Leicester was also a religious town with a multitude of different Christian sects. The democratic ethos of the chapels had also contributed to this tradition. During the mid-19th century many of these strands were subsumed into radical Liberalism which was to become the seed bed for the ideas of independent Labour representation and Socialism.

Manchester might be regarded as having been the capital of the retail Co-operative movement, but Leicester was the national centre for producers' co-operatives. The ability of these co-operatively run factories to sell to a thriving and developing network of co-op shops guaranteed the survival of most of them throughout the period of this book. These co-ops may not have been hugely significant in terms of Leicester's gross domestic product, but they were ideologically important in that they provided an alternative vision of society where working conditions were good, wages fair, profits shared and management accountable.

The existence of a working alternative economic system, based on Co-operative endeavour, was important in establishing the credibility of different social and political models. A few might have seen Co-operation as an alternative to trades unionism and Socialism. However, the evidence shows that local trade unions and trade unionists were instrumental in founding most co-operatives. There were conflicting attitudes towards Socialism and the role of the state, but these reflected the diversity of views then current within the Labour movement.

From Chartist times, the virtue of thrift and abstinence from drink was a strong influence on Labour movement activists. Although many early Socialists realised that drink was not the cause of poverty, but only a symptom of a deeper malaise, teetotalism (like anti-vaccination) remained significant for many in the local Labour movement.

Leicester's growth in the late 19th century stemmed from the expansion and mechanisation of the boot and shoe trade, supplementing an already established hosiery industry. The change to factory production and mechanisation during this period caused major changes to patterns of employment and resulted in the loss of craft occupation and the increased employment of women and boys. The conflicts caused by the forced pace of technological change helped create a generation of local Socialists and trade unionists.

There are very many significant occasions or subjects that no one thought to photograph or record visually. No daguerreotypes captured the mass agitation of Chartist times or leaders like John Markham. Mrs Mason, who organised a union for women outworkers in the 1880s, has left no visual record, nor has Leicester's Independent Union of Women Boot and Shoe Workers. However, we are lucky that one of the leaders of the 1905 Unemployed March was an amateur photographer.

This book cannot therefore claim to give a totally balanced history of either working-class life or politics in Leicester. It can offer a few snapshots, but not the whole picture. Many of the images in this volume have survived fortuitously and their inclusion inevitably colours our picture of the past. I have not limited the scope of this book to the confines of Leicester's city boundaries, but have nevertheless excluded Loughborough, Hinckley and Harborough as the latter have their own distinct histories.

Although the conditions of life in Leicester have changed, the desire for a more just society with opportunities for all remains a constant between then and now. The battle for women's suffrage has been won, the workhouses are long gone and the slums have been cleared, but the desire to overcome poverty and inequality in today's society should still be a guiding light for the Labour movement today.

Ned Newitt, October 2007

Acknowledgements

The photographs and other material in this book have come from a variety of different sources. Thanks are due to various individuals and organisations who have allowed me to use their precious items.

These include: Maggie Ash, Mr B. Bilson, David Bolton (Equity Shoes), Mark Crail, Malcolm Elliott, Neville Goodman, Rick Johnson (Leicester Carriage Builders), Martin Pantling, Mrs J. Setchfield, the Record Office for Leicestershire, Leicester and Rutland, Leicester Arts and Museum Service, the Leicester City Council Housing Department, the Independent Labour Party, the *Leicester Mercury*, Leicester South Labour Party, the Member Relations Department of the Midlands Co-operative Society, the National Archive, the Library of the London School of Economics and of the University of Leicester. I would also like to thank the staff at the Record Office for their courteous and expert assistance.

I am also very grateful to my wife Helen, who has often been abandoned during my research and writing, and who has also carefully corrected my numerous errors.

Above: Women workers in a Leicester boot and shoe factory.
Below left: A woman sewing shoe liners, c.1936.
Below right: A boot and shoe worker using a cement sole-attaching machine (made locally by the British United Shoe Machinery Company) at an unknown factory, c.1936.

PROCESSION

AND

PUBLIC MEETING.

The Council of the National Charter Association have great pleasure in announcing that

F. O'CONNOR

ESQ., M. P.,

WILL VISIT LEICESTER

ON MONDAY NEXT, MAY 8th,

When he will deliver a LECTURE in the Amphitheatre,

TO COMMENCE AT SEVEN O'CLOCK.

Subjects :---THE CHARTER---THE LAND, And the best means to obtain them.

ADMISSION, to the Boxes & Stage, 6d ; Pit 2d ; Gallery 1d. Members free to the Gallery on producing their Cards.

It is intended to meet Mr. F. O'Connor in Procession at the Railway Station. The Chartists in Town and County—the Land Companies—the Various Trades—and all who are friendly to the enfranchisement of the millions—are respectfully invited to take a part in the proceedings.

The Members and Friends of the National Charter Association are requested to meet in the Market Place, at ONE O'CLOCK. The unfortunate Stone-Breakers, near the Old Workhouse, Humberstone Gate—each Body to arrange themselves six abreast, and proceed to the Market Place.

At a quarter before Two o'clock, the Procession thus formed, will proceed down Humberstone Gate, up Charles-street, Northampton-street, and Foxe's-street, to meet Mr. O'Connor by the down train, at fifteen minutes past Two. Upon a given Signal, the Procession will again move on, taking the following route, viz., London Road, Belvoir-street, Welford Road, Oxford-street, Friar Lane, Market-place, (entering by the Fish Market,) High-street, North Gate-street, Sanvy Gate, Church Gate, Belgrave Gate, Woodboy-street, Wharf-street, Rutland-street, Granby-street, and Humberstone Gate.

☞ On Friday evening next, at Eight o'clock, the Council will be happy to meet Deputations from the Trades and other Bodies, at the Association Rooms, Hill Street, to give further instructions.

The Members of the National Land Company, who intend to form a distinct part in the procession, are requested to meet at the Office, Church Gate, at One o'clock.

N. B. Persons wishing to become Members of the National Charter Association, may enrol their names and obtain cards of membership at Mr. H. Green's, Grocer, Rutland-street, or from

W. H. Burton, Printer, London Road.

A Chartist poster from May 1848. When it became known that the Chartist leader Feargus O'Connor was to visit Leicester, some Tory magistrates attempted to ban the procession that was to meet him at the railway station. They were over-ruled by their Liberal colleagues, who trusted the moderation of the local Chartist leaders. Their trust was not misplaced as the procession and meeting passed off peacefully. William Jones, one of Leicester's Chartist poets, wrote a song for the occasion entitled Let Us Strive For The Charter.

'What cheers our 'lorn spirits when famished and pined?
When doomed to the stone-yard or sent forth to grind?
'Tis hope that our loved Charter we one day shall gain –
And we'll rally round it again and again!

However, a week later the town was thrown into disorder by the 'Bastille' riots. Three days of riot and alarm followed and it was only ended by the arrival of a company of the 87th Foot. The riots were a largely spontaneous reaction to the harshness of the Poor Law in the stone-yards and corn mills where the unemployed were put to work.

THOMAS COOPER,
AUTHOR OF "THE PURGATORY OF SUICIDES."

DRAWN BY H. ANELAY ; ENGRAVED BY H. LINTON.

Thomas Cooper: the Chartist

The 1831 Reform Act secured political influence for the middle classes. In Leicester, reformers who had supported universal (male) suffrage instead embraced the much-reviled Poor Laws. It was this that led to the establishment of Chartism in Leicester in 1838.

The Chartist agitation in Leicester lasted for almost 15 years. At its high points, the town saw mass agitation, strikes and demonstrations for the right to vote. Local Chartists linked the demands for an extension of the franchise to a campaign against the hated Poor Law and for better wages and conditions. In 1842 this campaign was met with repression, imprisonment and the use of troops against demonstrators.

Although Thomas Cooper had a great impact on local Chartism, he was only one of several Chartist leaders and was active in the town for only two years. Nevertheless, he was the only Leicester Chartist to attain anything like a national reputation.

> The time shall come when wrong shall end,
> When peasant to peer no more shall bend;
> When the lordly Few shall lose their sway,
> And the Many no more their frown obey.
> Toil, brothers, toil, till the work is done,
> Till the struggle is o'er, and the Charter won!
> *The Time Shall Come, c.1842*

His powerful speeches and poetry, his energy and drive and his colourful personality left an indelible impression on his contemporaries. Although he was an egotist and difficult to work with, his lasting influence was as an individual inspiration to the lives of other working men.

Cooper was arrested while visiting Burslem and was eventually sentenced to two years in Stafford prison for sedition. He was released in 1845, but did not return to Leicester.

Top left: Thomas Cooper.

Above left: The masthead of Leicester's short-lived Chartist newspaper: The Midland Counties Illuminator. *Its first editor, George Bown, was a veteran radical and a Jacobin in the 1790s who had been arrested for sedition. Its second editor was Thomas Cooper.*

Bottom left: An illustration from a handbill produced during the July 1837 parliamentary election. The Tory candidates Thomas Gladstone (brother of William) and Edward Goulburn are depicted as the comic actors, 'the drilled sergeant Mr Galleyborn and Mr Gallstone'. The Tories' opponents made much of the fact that Gladstone's father was a slave owner. The Liberal candidates were duly elected.

The hand stocking frame in the home. The decline of the hand operated knitting frames began in the 1880s. By the time this photograph was taken, c.1910, factories and powered machines had become dominant.

An old stockinger and his wife, who worked together for many years on stocking frames. Right: An undated handbill in verse, probably from the 1840s. The plight of the framework knitters during times of depression was the driving force behind Leicester Chartism.

THE
LEICESTERSHIRE FRAMEWORK-KNITTERS' PETITION.

PARDON our visit to this place,
And wait while we explain our case,
And then we think you'll pity take,
Nor us in our distress forsake.

Could we obtain our food by work
We'd labour like the hardy Turk;
But all our hopes from thence are fled,
And now we pine for want of bread.

Our children though to us most dear,
Must die for want we greatly fear,
Unless some humane gen'rous heart,
Some food for them to us import.

Could you our habitations see,
The seat of abject misery,
We think you would afford your aid,
Till we return unto our trade.

On heaven and you we now depend,
And trust in you we've found a friend;
And what you give God will repay,
Both here and in the judgement day.

J. Fowler, Printer, Leicester.

NOW IS THE TIME

MEN OF LEICESTER! ATTEND IN YOUR THOUSANDS!

Tomorrow, June 14,

when A

PUBLIC MEETING

will be held in the

MARKET PLACE,

At Eleven o'clock in the Morning,

For the purpose of shewing that the attempts of a base and corrupt faction to trample on the Rights and Liberties of Englishmen are vain and futile *and can no longer be toler- ated.* Let **Liberty, Equality,** and **Fraternity,** be your *Motto,* and the **Charter** and **No Surren- der** be your *rallying Cry.*

ASSEMBLE ! ASSEMBLE ! ASSEMBLE !

And give to your Friends in the Country an opportunity of joining you in the struggle for Freedom.

☞ *A new edition of the CHARTIST HYMN BOOK (containing a new Hymn for Chartist Camp Meetings) is now published at T. Warwick's Circulating Library, Union Street, price 3d. Edited by W. Jones, Leicester. Also, Sold by G. Buckby, No. 70, Lee Street; and J. W. Billson, News Agent, No. 13, Belgrave Gate, Leicester.*

T. WARWICK, PRINTER, UNION STREET, LEICESTER.

This poster from June 1848 was produced by Buckby's Workingmen's Association of Chartists. Using the pretext of rumours that men armed with pikes would attend, the advertised meeting was declared an unlawful assembly by the police. Although the above poster was used to cover over the police edicts pasted up round the town, the actual meeting was prevented from taking place.

Below: A membership card of the National Charter Association.

THOMAS RAYNER SMART.

George Buckby

George Buckby (above) was the most active local Chartist leader after 1846. He was a framework knitter and, with Thomas Smart, revived the movement following Thomas Cooper's impri- sonment. During the Chartist revival in 1848, Buckby was the Leicester delegate to the National Convention. His departure for London was made the occasion of a demonstration of over 7,000 Leicester Chartists behind a banner which proclaimed that 42,884 signatures to the petition had been obtained locally.

In the early 1850s, as secretary of the framework knitters, Buckby led the agitation against the fixed rent paid to middlemen for the hire of knitting frames. He petitioned Parliament for the abolition of frame rents and for legislation to give knitters protection against employers' frauds. He soon found himself victimised and in 1856 he took refuge in emigration to the United States, where he settled in Philadelphia.

Thomas Raynor Smart

Thomas Smart (left) was a Chartist leader and poet who was a delegate to the 1839 Chartist convention. He was born of working-class parents and died in 1847 aged 75. He was chief assistant to the Loughborough Chartist John Skevington until Smart moved to Leicester in 1842.

COME AND HEAR THE LIBERATED
BLASPHEMER!
MR. G. J. HOLYOAK,

Who has just been liberated from Six Months Imprisonment in Gloucester Gaol for the alleged offence of BLASPHEMY, will deliver a Course of

FOUR LECTURES,

IN THE

SOCIAL INSTITUTION, MARKET-PLACE, LEICESTER.

SUNDAY AFTERNOON, FEB. 26th, 1843,
Subject—"An attempt to explain MORAL CHARITY—a theme much talked of but little understood and practised."

SUNDAY EVENING,
"Christianity, as displayed in the recent Prosecution for Blasphemy—or a SHORT and EASY METHOD with the SAINTS."

MONDAY EVENING,
"The Formation and Publication of Opinions."

WEDNESDAY EVENING, FEBRUARY 29th,
"The Character of CHRISTIANS and the Duty of INFIDELS."

Admission to each Lecture 1d.

N.B.—A BALL will be held on TUESDAY, (SHROVE-TUESDAY EVENING,) at which Mr. H. will be present, and deliver a short Address.

J. WINDLEY, PRINTER & NEWS-AGENT, No. 8, CHURCH-GATE, LEICESTER.

G.J. Holyoake

G.J. Holyoake was an Owenite, Chartist, Secularist and pioneer of the Co-operative movement. Robert Owen's followers were early advocates of Socialism, free thinking and Co-operation. In Leicester, the Owenites went on to found the Secular Society. Holyoake had a close association with Leicester that lasted over 50 years. His meeting in Leicester was his first after being imprisoned for blasphemy. Later, he helped and advised the local Co-operative factories.

Left: William Holyoake (1818–1907) was an Owenite, poet and a founding member of the Secular Society in 1852. From 1846 he was both a tailor and bookseller. He later ran the Reform Bookstore at the Secular Hall from 1881 to 1902.

Below: The masthead of the short-lived working-class journal that published poetry from the pens of Leicester's Chartist and radical poets – notably William Jones.

Josiah Gimson

THE

LEICESTERSHIRE MOVEMENT, OR.

VOICES FROM THE FRAME AND THE FACTORY. THE FIELD AND THE RAIL, ETC.

| No. 1.—VOL. I. | SATURDAY, FEB. 9, 1850. | PRICE ONE PENNY. |

Josiah Gimson (1818–1881) was a former Owenite Socialist who became a follower of G.J. Holyoake. He was an engineer by trade and he eventually became a wealthy factory owner. He was the leader of the Leicester Secularists and the driving force behind the building of the Secular Hall. He was elected as a Liberal Councillor in 1877.

In the 1840s, Michael Wright (1818–1881) went to live and work in the unofficial Owenite Community at Manea Fen. By the 1860s he had become a prosperous manufacturer of elastic web, sometimes in conflict with the trade union. Opposed to theological teaching in schools, Wright helped to re-establish the Secular Society in 1867. In the 1870s he was active in the local Republican Association and became one of the leaders of the anti-vaccination movement. Wright was a total abstainer and a vegetarian.

Peter Alfred Taylor (1819–1891) was a Unitarian and member of the wealthy Courtauld family. He was elected as a Radical MP in 1862 to replace John Biggs. He was an advocate of universal suffrage and a republican, opposing public money being spent on royalty. In Parliament, Taylor worked closely with John Stuart Mill and Henry Fawcett in supporting women's suffrage.

John Biggs MP (1801–1871) with his nephew Arthur Biggs (1846–?), son of his brother William. This painting by an unknown artist probably dates from the mid-1850s.

John Biggs: the Radical hosier and MP

In the 1830s, John and William Biggs led the reform movement that swept the old corrupt Tory council from office. John Biggs became mayor three times. Although Radical in politics, he was not a Chartist and regarded unions as 'wrong-headed'. He saw free trade as the route to working-class improvement. In 1842 his Midland Counties Charter offered a 'moderate' alternative to the People's Charter. It proposed giving the vote to males over 25 and triennial parliaments. But the Chartists stood firm for their six points and any common ground between them was hampered by the middle-class manufacturers' disregard for working-class grievances. By the late 1840s, Biggs gained the support of former Chartists for an alliance that helped make the Liberals the dominant political force in the town. In the early 1850s, his standing with working-class radicals was enhanced when his firm voluntarily abolished practice of charging frame rents.

Biggs was elected to Parliament in June 1856 on the Reform Society's programme of votes by ballot, the redistribution of seats, triennial parliaments, the substitution of direct for indirect taxation and a national system of secular education. The former Chartist leader John Markham became one of his allies on the Town Council while the ex-Chartist leader Buckby advised his followers to vote Radical.

Thomas Emery: a Radical Editor

The Grand Old Man of the Trade Union and Co-op movement.

Daniel Merrick

Thomas Emery (1820–1868) was a self-made man who helped ensure working-class support for radical Liberalism in Leicester. During the 1850s he acted as a bridge between the Liberal Party, ex-Chartists and trade unionists.

In the 1840s Emery was a supporter of Robert Owen and, in 1850, he published a pamphlet on education arguing for the provision of compulsory state secular education. In 1852 he was one of the founders of the Leicester Secular Society, though he later became a Unitarian.

Emery came from a working-class background and had started work as a glove hand. By 1852 he was running a bookshop in Belgrave Gate and in 1855 he became the founding editor of the *South Midlands Free Press*. He used the paper to support Radicalism and the Liberal cause. In 1861 he was part of a delegation of 'extreme Liberals' who successfully invited the radical P.A. Taylor to stand for Parliament. During the American Civil War, Emery gave his paper's support to the Northern cause against slavery.

Daniel Merrick (1821–1888) was a stockinger and leader of the Sock and Top Union. He took part in the Chartist agitation and was a member of Thomas Cook's short-lived co-operative society that sold potatoes and flour. He was a member of the first Co-operative Hosiery Manufacturing Society, formed in 1867, and when the society failed he helped it continue in business under the auspices of his hosiery union.

In 1870 he was elected to the School Board and then became the first working man to be elected to the Town Council. At the time there was a £1,000 property qualification for councillors. Although Merrick had little money, a sum of £1,000 was paid into his account by his admirers. In 1871 he initiated the working-class based Democratic Association that soon became the Republican Association.

In 1872 he became the first president of the Leicester and District Trades Council and in 1885 he became president of the Leicester Co-operative Society.

Leicester Co-operative Society founders and first committee, c.1860. Left to right: J. Woodford, G. Sharpe, G. Herbert, T. Norton (secretary), S. Wilford, H.C. Burrows, E. Silverwood.

The Leicester Co-operative Society sprang from a meeting at Mr Woodford's house at 15 Brook Street, Wharf Street, in 1859.

The Early Years of the Leicester Co-op

The Leicester Co-operative Society was founded in 1859 by seven workers at Wheeler's Abbey Mills factory on Ross Walk. They wanted to have a shop where food was not adulterated, where the profits were returned to the customers and the prices were reasonable. At their first meeting they each put threepence into a fund and within a month they had 10s in capital.

Slowly the capital and membership increased and, in July 1860, they registered the 'Leicester Industrial Co-operative Society'. Two months later they opened a shop at 15 Belgrave Gate, nearly opposite the present day Argos store. Where previous attempts to form Co-operative societies in Leicester had failed, the Belgrave Gate shop succeeded.

Members had to have paid 10 shillings into the society before they could share in the dividends or vote at business meetings. When a member made a purchase, it was entered into a little book by the 'shopman'. The purchases were then totalled up by a committee member and the profits divided according to how much you had bought.

In 1866 the society decided on a bold experiment and opened a branch shop at 2 Sanvey Gate. It was so successful that other branches soon followed. In October 1867 the society rented a bakehouse in Friars Causeway, and in May of the next year it opened a second bakehouse at the rear of the Marble Street branch. A warehouse and office were purchased and in 1871 a drapery business was started in Bond Street. Between 1872 and 1876, 12 new branches were opened. A butchers was established at the corner of High Street and Highcross Street and five new branch butchers were quickly opened. The Leicester Co-operative Society was now a major retail force in the town.

A Co-op Pioneer

By virtue of his education, Thomas Norton (above) became the leader of the web weavers who founded the Leicester Co-operative Society. He became secretary of the society and the manager of its first shop at 15 Belgrave Gate. In the days before the CWS, he had to tour the country to buy produce. He had responsibility for the society's cash box and kept it in his house. With much poverty and unemployment in the town, there was a serious problem of crime and burglary. The cash could not be let out of his sight. When he went for a Sunday afternoon walk the cash box came too, disguised as a parcel. Norton remained secretary until his resignation in 1876. He lived to see the jubilee of the society in 1910.

The first branch store at 2 Sanvey Gate opened in July 1866. The opening of branches in the densely populated parts of town was long debated by the society's board. One member, having belonged to the Chartist Feargus O'Connor's ill-fated land scheme, was adamant that opening another branch would doom the society to failure. Eventually, his caution was overcome and the society rapidly expanded.

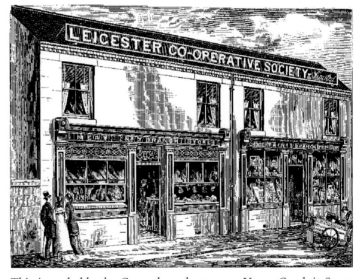

This is probably the Co-op branch store on Upper Conduit Street, sometime after 1876.

Right: The publication of the Leicester Co-operative Record started in 1874 and continued into the 1920s, when it was replaced by the Leicester Co-operative Magazine. *It provided news and information about the retail business and the local producer Co-operative factories.*

LEICESTER CO-OPERATIVE RECORD.

LET·EACH·MAN·FIND·HIS·OWN·IN·ALL·MENS·GOOD   AND·ALL·MEN·WORK·IN·NOBLE·BROTHERHOOD.

No. 187.]   MAY, 1889.   [Gratis.

By the mid-1870s, the Leicester Co-operative Society had 27 branches, and a central warehouse and store. In 1875 John Butcher (the CWS boot works manager) persuaded a reluctant board to purchase a block of property at the corner of High Street and Union Street. The land was bought for £9,800 and plans were drawn up by the architect Thomas Hind. Hind was an active Co-operator, member of the board and town councillor. The new Central Store, Co-operative Hall and central administration was opened on 10 November 1884.

Leicester Co-operative Society General Board, 1875. Top row: J. Broome, E. Dadley, H. Harriott, T. Hind, W. Green, I. Abbott, J. Warren. Bottom row: J. Butcher, A. Lythall, J.H. Wyman, T. Norton (secretary), B. Hemmings (president), J. Banbury (treasurer), J. Staples, H. Underwood.

The CWS boot and shoe factory on Duns Lane in 1876. This was the second CWS factory in the country.

CWS manager John Butcher.

*The Duns Lane factory c.1904,
after it had been extended.*

John Butcher was born to a Northampton shoemaking family. During his early life he was a staunch Radical and a follower of the Chartist Ernest Jones. Having risen to prominence in the Co-operative Wholesale Society, he became the driving force behind the expansion of Co-operation in Leicester in the 1870s. The CWS was already manufacturing biscuits and he told its board that 'biscuits were a luxury and boots were a necessity'. On this advice, the CWS opened a boot factory in Leicester on Duns Lane in September 1873 that initially employed 100 people. Managed by Butcher, the West End works rapidly expanded and became the principal supplier of footwear to every retail society in the country. Butcher was a Liberal Town Councillor from 1883–91, a member of the board of the Leicester Co-operative Society and also of the Leicester Co-operative Hosiery Manufacturing Society.

Messrs Healey, Newell & Bodicoat, three of the original shareholders and current workers in 1898.

George Newell: Trade Unionist and Co-operative Manager

George Newell was a framework knitter and in the early 1870s, along with Daniel Merrick, he was a leader of the Sock and Top Union. This union amalgamated with two other branches and unions to form the Leicester and Leicestershire Framework Knitters' Union and Newell became its secretary. In 1875 the union bought out a failing hosiery producers' co-operative that had been started in 1867. The union members were not unanimous about running a workshop and the venture did not prosper.

In 1876 a second hosiery manufacturing co-operative was started and Newell was appointed its general manager. The Leicester Second Co-operative Hosiery Manufacturing Society began using hand frames, and in 1882 it expanded and moved factory premises, where powered machinery was introduced. In 1890, the Co-op moved to the Cranbourne Street Mills. Newell worked as manager until his death and contemporary reports speak of the very congenial

The Cranbourne Street Mills, c.1903.

working conditions in the factory. The success of this venture was to prove the inspiration for other local producer co-ops.

Newell developed a close affinity with the national Co-op pioneer Edward Greening and the Christian Socialist E.V. Neale. Newell was a deacon at the Oxford Street Chapel and he saw Co-operative production as a means of applying Christian principles to industrial life. He eventually became the spokesman for the Producers' Co-operative Federation and was a Liberal town councillor from 1899–1901.

In 1903, the CWS attempted to buy out the Hosiery Society. Initially this met with some strong opposition, but the resistance eventually crumbled and the factory passed to the CWS in July 1903. In 1908, the CWS transferred the Leicester hosiery production to a new factory in Huthwaite, Nottinghamshire. The following year the Cranbourne Street factory commenced production as a CWS box-making and print works. The factory was extended in 1913.

Above: George Newell (1849–1901).
Left: The trade mark of the Co-operative Hosiery Society. 'Symergon' was pronounced Ce-mer-gun and meant 'Co-operative working together'.

An interior photograph of the Cranbourne Street factory of the Co-operative Hosiery Manufacturing Society, c.1898. In this room workers made shirts, pants and drawers, women's vests and combinations on linkers and Cotton's Patent machines.

The long room, in 1898, at the Cranbourne Street factory. This room housed the Cotton's Patent machines that were used to manufacture children's cashmere, cotton shirts, socks, plain hose and pants and drawers. In 1864, William Cotton of Loughborough had devised a method of machine-knitting fabric whereby it could be shaped or fashioned automatically, and all machines that embody this principle are known as 'Cotton's Patent'.

'The workers at Cranbourne Mill recognise the unity of the Co-operative movement, and the necessity and pleasure of giving intelligent and hearty service so that their fellow Co-operators may be served as well or better than any private capitalist can serve them.' – *Distributive Co-operation in Leicester,* 1898.

The Cardigan Room, c.1898, at the Cranbourne Street factory. This room produced sweaters, men's and women's cardigans and women's and children's rib vests.

The workroom for making women's and children's rib cashmeres on Cotton Patents.

'Every man, or woman, or society member may nominate and vote for each one of the Committee and President. They do not have to attend a meeting to do this, as the papers are sent to each member to be filled and returned. Upon the Board of Management there must be Two Workers, Four representatives of the Distributive Stores, Six Individuals and a President. They have 323 Distributive Society members, who own nearly two-thirds of the capital.'

Distributive Co-operation in Leicester, 1898.

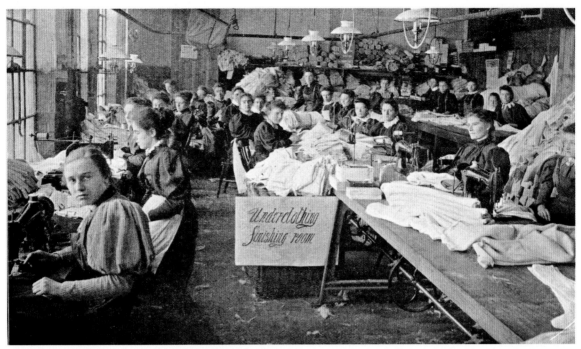

Machinists at work in the 'underclothing' finishing room.

The 'New Room' at the Cranbourne Street factory. After the CWS switched hosiery production out of Leicester, Cranbourne Street remained in use as a CWS printing works for more than 50 years.

'There are a large proportion of women and girls employed in the factory, and as I was passing through I heard many a snatch of a hymn, with an occasional chorus; and when I can hear the melody of human voices rising above the noise of mill machinery…I need no further evidence to convince me that the iron has not entered into the souls of the singers…Give me a class of work-people who can sing and dare sing, in the presence of their manager and strangers, and I will give you the character of the place at which they are employed…'

The Workman's Times.

The Griswold room at the Cranbourne Street factory. The Griswold machines made the seamless type of hose, half hose and socks. From the 1870s it became possible to produce patterned goods, especially one-by-one rib-knitted stockings or ribbed goods (e.g. socks with an attached rib border) with a machine patented by the American D. Griswold. The machine even made it possible to knit continuous tubes of stockings. In 1881 Griswold formed the London and Leicester Hosiery Company Ltd to purchase his patents and manufacture and to sell his machines. Improvements to Griswold knitters were soon made by other manufacturers.

A tour of inspection by the Co-operative Women's Guild Midlands Conference, visiting the hosiery works on Tuesday 16 February 1892.

Hand-frame knitters at work in a factory, c.1900. These were hand-powered machines whose lineage dates back to the 16th century.

Jimmy Holmes (1850–1911)

James Holmes (left) entered the hosiery trade as a winding boy, progressing from hand frames to machines. By the mid-1880s he had operated every kind of knitting machine then in existence. In the mid-1870s he was elected to the executive of the Framework Knitters' Union, and became an official of the union in 1881.

Holmes was an exceptional organiser and a powerful orator. In the late 1870s he was a prolific lecturer to the Secular Society, only to later become a spiritualist. In the 1880s, Holmes was a friend of Tom Barclay and was probably a member of the Socialist League. He was a founder member of the ILP in the 1890s and was a supporter of the Co-operative movement. He was a member of the TUC parliamentary committee in the late 1880s and a shareholder in the Leicester Pioneer Press in the 1900s.

His life ended in disgrace when it was discovered, as he lay dying of cancer, that he had embezzled union funds on a grand scale, investing in about 200 houses in and around Leicester. They were all heavily mortgaged and the union realised little on their sale. One admirer of Holmes described this as 'a sad ending to a brilliant and honourable career in the championship of Labour'.

The Boot and Shoe Union Founded

The Amalgamated Cordwainers' Association represented the traditional hand-sewn shoe workers, whose craft had remained unchanged for centuries. Its members tended to look down on the newcomers in the machine-made trade and this spurred the formation of the breakaway union. In 1873, 25 men founded the National Union of Boot and Shoe Rivetters and Finishers as a breakaway.

By 1876 the new union, whose members called themselves 'The Sons of St Crispin', was able to establish a funeral fund and offer sick pay of 10 shillings a week. With over 1,300 members in Leicester, the town was chosen for the new union's 'seat of government'. An HQ was established in Cranbourne Street and it was not long before union officials began to make themselves felt in the town's civic life as Liberal Party supporters.

In 1874 Thomas Smith (1847–1919) became the first general secretary of the Boot and Shoe Union. His position in the trade union movement gained him prominence in the Liberal Party and in 1877 he was elected to the School Board. In the following year he resigned his secretaryship of the union to become the full-time secretary of the Leicester Liberal Association.

Following the Conciliation Act of 1896, he was appointed by the Board of Trade as Conciliator and acted as arbitrator in many trade disputes in different parts of the country. He was also a town councillor and in 1907 he became the first mayor from a trade union and working-class background. (See below.)

A shoemaker working at home in the late 19th century, using traditional methods of hand sewing.

George Sedgwick, 1846–1934, (right) was also a founder of NUBSO. He became general secretary in 1878 and was a supporter of arbitration. Sedgwick believed that many strikes could easily be settled if men and employers could meet and talk. He saw the union's role 'as a mediator between employers and workmen in trade disputes'. He was a member of the School Board 1879–1886 and was one of the first working men appointed as an inspector of factories.

A membership certificate for the newly formed Boot and Shoe Union dated 1874. Eventually it became known as the National Union of Boot and Shoe Operatives (NUBSO). St Crispin was the patron saint of boot and shoe workers and St Crispin's day (25 October) was frequently marked by rowdy celebrations. There is a record of the motto 'May the Trade Be Trodden Underfoot by the Whole World' being used on a banner of the Nantwich shoemakers in 1834.

Pledge cards of this kind (above) were a campaigning tool of the Temperance movement. The association of publicans with the Tory party was made initially by the Liberals and then by the Socialists in their appeal to the 'respectable' working classes.

The Leicester Unionist Working Men's Club as seen by our artist on Friday last week. He was particularly struck with the adroit way in which Sir John Rolleston and the Right Hon. George Wyndham, M.P., pumped up and distributed the various Tory liquors that were on tap. [See his remarks elsewhere.]

Temperance

The Temperance movement was especially strong in Leicester. It had been an active strand of Chartism where supporters were encouraged to take the pledge until the Charter had been won. It remained an influence within the Labour movement up until 1939.

Although some in the churches and Liberal party saw drink as the sole cause of poverty, many early Socialists were also advocates of temperance.

Leicester Pioneer, 1908.

Henry Matts, jailed for 30 days in 1871.

George Frith, jailed for 14 days in 1872.

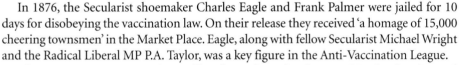

Above and below: The huge Anti-Vaccination demonstration in the Market Place in March 1885. Right: Some of the people jailed for refusing to have their children vaccinated.

The Anti-Vaccination League

Leicester was at the forefront of the campaign against compulsory smallpox vaccination. Starting in the 1860s, the movement lasted for over 30 years. The campaign embraced all parties and was pursued with an almost religious fervour, attracting great popular support.

'Compulsory vaccination, in a matter so closely affecting the tenderest and deepest feelings of parents, was regarded as a Poll Tax, of an even more obnoxious character than that which occasioned the uprising of 1381…' J.T. Biggs, 1911.

Joseph Wright, jailed for 14 days in 1872.

In 1876, the Secularist shoemaker Charles Eagle and Frank Palmer were jailed for 10 days for disobeying the vaccination law. On their release they received 'a homage of 15,000 cheering townsmen' in the Market Place. Eagle, along with fellow Secularist Michael Wright and the Radical Liberal MP P.A. Taylor, was a key figure in the Anti-Vaccination League.

There were 6,037 prosecutions of local people under the 1867 Vaccination Act and 64 people were sent to prison. In 1885, thousands of protestors marched from the Temperance Hall to the Market Place where copies of the Vaccination Acts were burnt in full view of the Mayor and Chief Constable. This demonstration led to a Royal Commission that sat for seven years. Its 1896 report concluded that vaccination protected against smallpox, but as a gesture to the anti-vaccinationists it recommended the abolition of cumulative penalties. A new Vaccination Act in 1898 introduced a conscience clause, allowing parents who did not believe vaccination was safe to obtain exemption. This introduced the concept of the 'conscientious objector' into English law.

Charles Eagle, jailed for 10 days in 1876.

William Ball, jailed for 14 days in 1883.

Vaughan Working Men's College, Great Central Street.

Revd David Vaughan.

Adult Schools and Adult Education

Economic necessity meant children started work at an early age. Despite the introduction of compulsory schooling in 1870, most people's education remained rudimentary. Many of the leaders and activists in the Labour movement had to struggle to gain some education. Both the Owenites and Chartists had run schools during the 1840s, and in 1846 Joseph Dare's mission to the poor took over the old Chartist room at All Saints Open, Highcross Street. The discussion classes held there were to influence many early working-class radicals. The classes at the Leicester Working Men's Institute became essential to those bent on self-improvement. Founded in 1862 by the Reverend David Vaughan and his wife Margaret, it was later renamed Vaughan Memorial College.

Many were active in the Adult School movement and the later Worker's Educational Association among others. Local Co-operatively run factories ran programmes of education for their workers, while the Leicester Co-operative Society has provided adult education throughout its history.

Leicester Working Men's College in Union Street, 1862–69.

The spacious education room at the Leicester Co-operative Hosiery Society, Cranbourne Street, c.1898.

Women Elected

Fanny Fullagar (1847–1918) was the first woman in Leicester to be elected to public office. She was the daughter of a Belvoir Street doctor and, despite being engaged for seven years, never married. In the 1880s she became active in the campaign for women's suffrage.

As the result of a court case, it became possible for women to stand for election to the Board of Guardians (which ran the local workhouses) if they were property owners. In 1888 Fanny Fullagar was elected to the Board of Guardians as a Liberal candidate. She was later joined by several other middle-class Liberal women, including Charlotte Ellis and Dorothy Coy.

Above and below: Some of the inmates of the Swain Street Institution or 'bassy' or bastille, as it was it was known. To the poor, the workhouse represented the ultimate punishment for poverty. Despite their presence on the Board of Guardians, the Liberal women did little to challenge some of the fundamental injustices in the Poor Law system, such as the labour test, oakhum picking, the separation of the sexes and the use of cells.

Old Stockingers, Inmates of the Leicester Union Workhouse.

Left: Edith Gittins (1845–1910) founded the Leicester Women's Liberal Association in 1886, at a time when women had no political power, and was its leader for many years. She was also the mainstay of the Leicester Women's Suffrage Society and was an unusual combination of artist and social reformer. She was a disciple of Ruskin and Morris and exhibited at the Royal Academy. She taught at the Unitarian Great Meeting Sunday School for 40 years.

John Potter (1847–1907) was president of 'Equity Shoes' for 18 years. He was a key figure in the whole of the Co-operative enterprise in Leicester, being also on the board of the Leicester Co-operative Printing Society and advisor to the Anchor Society. He was a Liberal, a Secularist and a member of the School Board.

H. H. Woolley (born 1859), along with his father and brother, was among the initiators of Equity Shoes. He was an active union member and in 1891 he became an official of NUBSO. He became a pioneer of Independent Labour representation when in 1893 he was elected to the Council as the Trades Council candidate independently from the Liberal party. His father Joseph Woolley was already a Liberal councillor. Both were Secularists.

Equity Shoes

Leicester Co-operative Boot and Shoe Manufacturing Society or 'Equity Shoes' was founded in 1886 as the result of a strike at the CWS factory. Following the dispute, the strike committee decided to set up their own factory, manage it themselves and share in the profits. They started business with £420 in capital that had been contributed by the workers themselves, their trade union and a few sympathisers. At first, Equity could only employ four workers and had to compete with the larger and better-equipped CWS factory. Initially, jobs that the CWS did by machine, Equity did by hand, but progress was rapid. By 1895, Equity employed 280 workers and had built a new factory on Western Road, where it is still in business.

The first premises of the Leicester Co-operative Boot and Shoe Manufacturing Society on Friars Causeway in 1886.

The press room at the Leicester Co-operative Boot and Shoe Works second factory at Bede Street, Leicester, in October 1890.

The closing room at the Leicester Co-operative Boot and Shoe Works at Bede Street, Leicester, in October 1890.

The 'Educational Institute' on the top floor of the Leicester Co-operative Boot and Shoe Works second factory at Bede Street, Leicester, in February 1890. This hall seated 250 people and newspapers, games, a piano (of Co-operative make) and a library were available to the workforce.

Above: An advert for Equity shoes from 1910.
Top left: The works entrance to the Equity factory on Western Road as it is today.
Bottom left: Equity's Western Road factory was opened in 1896 and extended in 1898.

THE SECULAR HALL, LEICESTER.

SUNDAY FREE LECTURES,

The following LECTURES will be
delivered on Sunday Evenings,

IN THE

SECULAR HALL

Commencing at 6.30.

1889   SUBJECT.

Jan. 6   Mr. F. W. READ---"The Philosophy of Individualism."

" 13   Mrs. MARY SOWDEN { "The Origin and Growth of Religions as illustrated by the Ancient Babylonians."

" 20   Mr. GRAHAM WALLAS---"Property under Socialism."

" 27   Mr. F. FEROZA---"The claims of Phrenology."

Feb. 3   Mr. F. MILLAR---"The Politics of Individualism."

" 10   Mrs. ANNIE BESANT { "The organization of Industry under Socialism."

" 17   Mr. WORDSWORTH DONISTHORPE "The Limits of Liberty."

" 24   Mr. ALFRED MILNES, M.A.---"The Rights of the Individual."

Mar. 3   Mr. HUBERT BLAND---"The Outlook of Socialism."

" 10   ANNIVERSARY SERVICES { when many old friends in the Secularist movement will attend and speak.

ADMISSION FREE.

DISCUSSION INVITED.

SECULAR HALL,

LEICESTER.

On Wednesday, January 23, 1884,

Mr. Wm. MORRIS,

(Author of "The Earthly Paradise," &c., and Treasurer of the Democratic Federation), will

LECTURE

IN THE SECULAR HALL, ON

"ART AND SOCIALISM."

DISCUSSION IS INVITED.

The Lectures will begin at 8 p.m.   Doors open at 7.30.

A portion of the Hall will be reserved for holders of Tickets, price One Shilling each, which can be obtained from the Secular Hall Bookstall, GEO. GIBBONS & Co., King Street, or from Mr. BENT, Town Hall Lane.

To other parts of the Hall, **ADMISSION FREE.**

The REV. J. PAGE HOPPS will Lecture in the Secular Hall, on Monday, January 28th, on Socialism; in opposition to the proposals of Messrs. HYNDMAN and MORRIS.

GEO. GIBBONS & Co., Printers, 47, King Street, Leicester.

The Secular Hall

The Secular Hall, designed by William Larner Sugden in the style of the Flemish Renaissance, opened in 1881. It was largely financed by the former Owenite Socialists Josiah Gimson and Michael Wright. During the 1860s and 1870s Charles Bradlaugh's oratory brought new recruits to Secularism on the issues of the extension of the franchise, Republicanism and birth control.

During the 1880s, the Leicester Secular Society played a key role in fostering new political ideas by inviting the advanced thinkers of the day to lecture. In 1884, the Marxist H.M. Hyndman and William Morris spoke about their ideas of Socialism. Morris's lecture in particular made a deep impression and won many followers, including Secularist Tom Barclay, who wrote:

'Chartism was dead and no one knew anything of the Socialism of the times of Robert Owen. Many thought the abolition of the monarchy would put us all right…About 1883, the Bradlaugh v. Hyndman debate in St James Hall London, inclined many thoughtful people to Socialism. The Fabian Society sprang up and the Secular Society was the first in Leicester to invite their speakers and expounders…Sidney Webb, Hubert Bland, Mrs Besant, William Morris and Bernard Shaw.'

The Secular Hall c.1894. The portraits on the balcony are of (left to right): G.J. Holyoake, Josiah Gimson, Charles Bradlaugh MP, Michael Wright and Tom Slater (the hall's former manager).

Above: A Socialist League poster from 1889.

Tom Barclay – Leicester's Socialist Pioneer

Tom Barclay (1852–1933) was born in a two-roomed hovel in a court off Burley's Lane in Leicester's Irish district. His parents had been starved out of Ireland by the potato famine. Tom never went to school and was taught to read by his mother. Although he scraped along in various menial jobs for most of his life, he had a profound influence on the intellectual life of the city.

He loved literature, especially Ruskin, and he felt an obvious empathy with William Morris. Barclay saw capitalism as evil and he despised the moral and spiritual degradation that it created. In November 1885 he helped found the Leicester branch of the Socialist League and wrote for Morris's *Commonweal* newspaper.

During his life he was a member of the Social Democratic Federation, the Anarchists and the Independent Labour Party, but he disliked the sectarianism of the left of those days. He claimed to have influenced many of the founders of the ILP, and c.1892 he founded the *Leicester Pioneer*, a newspaper exclusively for the Labour movement, while he also contributed accounts of the Leicester slums to *The Wyvern*.

Over a period of 50 years he claimed to have worked in 20 factories, spending the last 25 years of his life working mainly as a bottle-washer. Throughout his life he had an insatiable thirst for knowledge. He was a true working-class intellectual and free thinker.

'And now we began to meet – "we few against the world" – to address the "many headed monster thing" from trolley platforms in all the different squares in Leicester. Every Sunday twice and sometimes two or three week nights. We preached and exhorted: we formed classes: we sold literature: we challenged opponents: we held debates: we collected coppers to pay the train fare of speakers from other towns' – Tom Barclay.

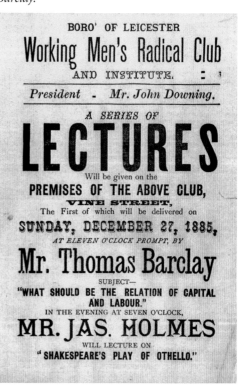

This picture, taken in the late 1920s, shows two-roomed houses in Burley's Yard with their shared outside toilets. Tom Barclay was born in a court off Burley's Lane in 1852.

The junction of Abbey Street and Mansfield Street in the late 1920s. Following the famine in Ireland, this area became home to Leicester's Irish community. During his childhood, Tom Barclay's family lived in a nearby court and in 1895 Barclay described the lodging house (below) as being kept by a 'quiet widow who would not have the drunkard and the rowdy inside her door if she knows it. The rooms are plentifully furnished with draws and crockery; on one wall is a picture of the Crucifixion, on another the ascension of Mary into heaven…Fascinating Irish girls march up and down outside with nothing on their heads and everybody sits outside the door these evenings.'

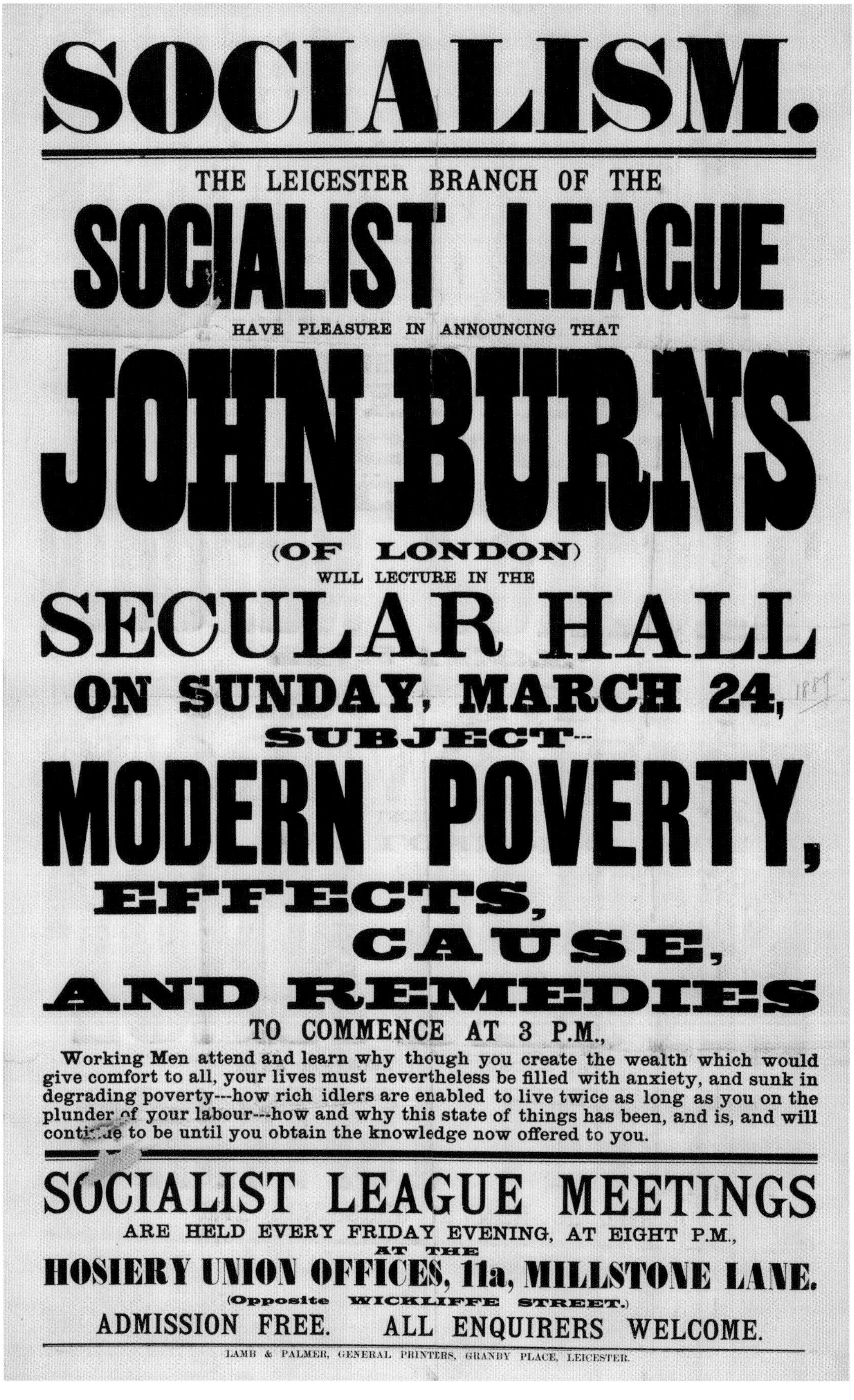

SOCIALISM.

THE LEICESTER BRANCH OF THE

SOCIALIST LEAGUE

HAVE PLEASURE IN ANNOUNCING THAT

JOHN BURNS

(OF LONDON)

WILL LECTURE IN THE

SECULAR HALL

ON SUNDAY, MARCH 24, 1889

SUBJECT--

MODERN POVERTY,

EFFECTS,

CAUSE,

AND REMEDIES

TO COMMENCE AT 3 P.M.,

Working Men attend and learn why though you create the wealth which would give comfort to all, your lives must nevertheless be filled with anxiety, and sunk in degrading poverty---how rich idlers are enabled to live twice as long as you on the plunder of your labour---how and why this state of things has been, and is, and will continue to be until you obtain the knowledge now offered to you.

SOCIALIST LEAGUE MEETINGS

ARE HELD EVERY FRIDAY EVENING, AT EIGHT P.M.,

AT THE

HOSIERY UNION OFFICES, 11a, MILLSTONE LANE.

(Opposite WICKLIFFE STREET.)

ADMISSION FREE.   ALL ENQUIRERS WELCOME.

LAMB & PALMER, GENERAL PRINTERS, GRANBY PLACE, LEICESTER.

The Early Socialists

During the 1880s, Socialism in Leicester consisted of a small branch of William Morris's Socialist League, whose members were mainly young hosiery workers and Secularists. It was little more than a propaganda organisation, since it refused to take part in elections. By the 1890s the local branch had veered towards Anarchism, enabling Hyndman's Social Democratic Federation and the Christian Socialists to grow in influence.

However, the mainstream of working-class political activity was conducted under the aegis of the Liberal Party. In the early 1890s, Socialism began to find support within the Boot and Shoe Union and it was from this base that demands for independent Labour representation began to grow.

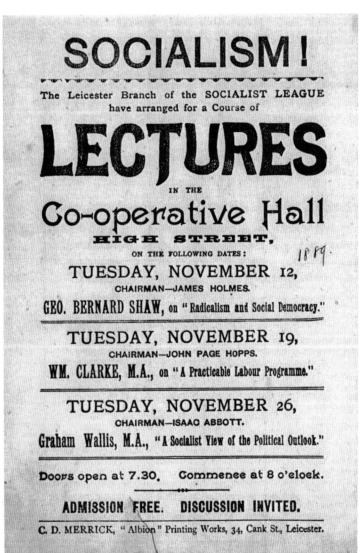

Above: The Socialist League programme for November 1889.
Left: Archibald Gorrie (c.1856–1941) was secretary of the Socialist League in 1889.

Archibald Gorrie was a draper and was 'converted' to Socialism after listening to Tom Barclay speaking from the back of a dray in Humberstone Gate. He often paid for the rent of a hall, the printing of posters or a speaker's expenses. He was an active Christian Socialist, Anarchist and passive resister to the religious clauses of the 1902 Education Act. He later joined the Independent Labour Party and was elected to the Board of Guardians. In the 1930s he was a Labour councillor.

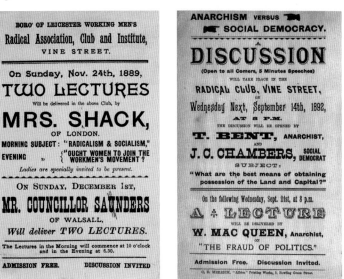

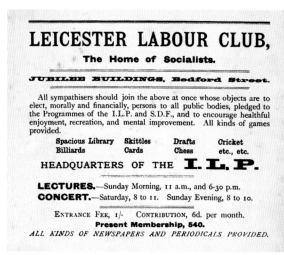

The Socialist and Labour Club

As trade unionists began to take an interest in Socialism, a club was formed that brought all the various Socialist groups, individuals and trade unionists together under one roof. The Socialist and Labour Club organised the first May Day demonstration in 1893 and this event, under the auspices of the Trades Council, soon became the annual rally of the trade union movement.

At the first rally, Joseph Potter caused something of a stir when he told the crowd that the local Liberal MP, Picton, had been 'a parson and was a capitalist. They might as well send a leopard in sheep's clothing amongst a flock of sheep as send a capitalist to represent the workers in Parliament'.

In 1894 the club invited Keir Hardie, of the newly-formed ILP, to Leicester (see right) and in 1896 a second club was opened on Millstone Lane.

Above: Leicester's first May Day rally, 1893.

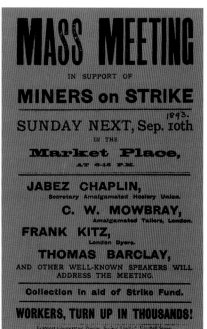

The speakers on this platform included a Liberal (Chaplin) and a London Anarchist (Kitz).

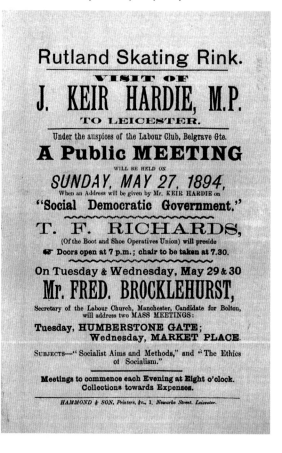

Independent Labour Representation

In March 1894, Leicester's two Liberal MPs decided to retire. Although the ex-trade union leader Henry Broadhurst was put forward as a Liberal-Labour candidate, the other Liberal nomination was unacceptable to the Socialists on the Trades Council.

Their leader, T.F Richards, wrote to Keir Hardie to ask him to stand an Independent Labour Party candidate in Leicester. Hardie agreed, with the proviso that a local ILP branch was started after the election. Tom Mann was promptly sent to Leicester to win over the Trades Council in support of Joseph Burgess, the hastily nominated ILP candidate.

Tom Mann's speech to the Trades Council was so effective that George Banton, president of the council and a Liberal committee member, joined the ILP, becoming the first president of the Leicester Branch.

The rush to hold the poll left little time for preparation and Burgess did not arrive in Leicester until four days before the vote. Burgess and Mann were joined by Keir Hardie to wage a spirited campaign that gained 4,402 votes. This election established the ILP in the town and the Liberal Association's working-class support had begun to wane.

Joseph Burgess c.1896.

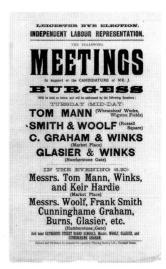

An ILP handbill from the 1894 bye-election advertising meetings with the big names of British Socialism.

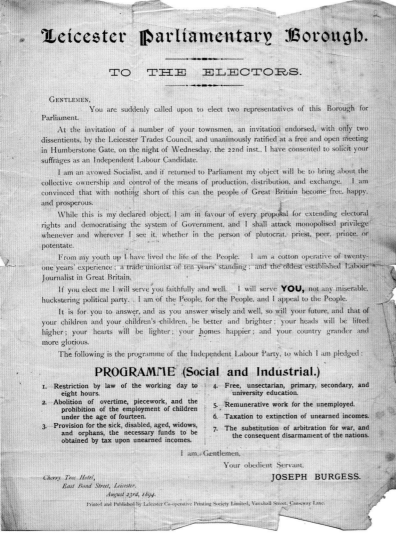

Above: Joseph Burgess's election address of August 1894.

George Banton was the President of the ILP 1894–1909 and was elected to the Town Council in 1896. He later became MP for Leicester East.

December 1894 – Municipal Success for the ILP

'We set to work and our opponents say we do work. We paraded the ward with a home made lantern three feet square and set upon two poles, with mottoes on each side, and a naphtha lamp inside, and accompanied by our ILP brass band. More canvas, more votes, and whilst we are canvassing we are making Socialists, which is our principal object and we insist upon a good energetic canvas. Whilst one person is doing this and addressing circulars, the agitators are holding fifteen to twenty meetings, and we make a point of holding a meeting in each street of the ward, and often four or five upon a good central spot. On polling day we see that all vote and give them no peace until they do.'
The Wyggeston Ward Election, Freddy Richards, 3 December 1898.

By the early 1900s, the ILP's electioneering was achieving some modest success at council elections, forcing the Liberals to adopt similar tactics.

The ILPs Municipal Programme, 1894

Freddy Richards was a key figure in the founding of the local ILP. He was also the first local ILP councillor, elected in December 1894.

Municipal Bye-Election.

To the Electors of Wyggeston Ward.

FELLOW BURGESSES,

I am again requested by a large number of Burgesses and Friends of this Ward to place my services at your disposal as an INDEPENDENT LABOUR CANDIDATE, and, after considering the generous manner with which you supported the Labour cause, I ask you for a renewal of that confidence, and trust that the 718 votes recorded will this time be double that number. Being a *bond-fide* working man, I claim to understand the wants and requirements of the workers much better than moneyed men who live by usury, and should you honour me with your confidence I promise to give a yearly account of my stewardship, and will endeavour to carry out the following

I.L.P. PROGRAMME,

Submitted and approved at a General Meeting of the I.L.P., Co-operative Hall,
——*October 22nd, 1894.*——

1.—Labour Newspapers and Magazines to be placed in the Town Free Libraries.

2.—All Representatives to be paid for their services, and the official expenses of election out of the borough rates.

3.—Municipalisation of Tramways, 'Busses, and other vehicles plying for hire.

4.—The construction by the Corporation of Working Men's healthy Dwellings, in proportion to the needs of the population, such dwellings to be let at rent to cover the cost of construction and maintenance, with a reasonable proportion set on one side for sinking fund.

5.—Abolition of the Contract and Sub-Contract system. All Labour, where possible, to be employed direct by the Municipal or other local bodies ; and

that Trades Union rates of wages and conditions be conformed to.

6.—As one means of absorbing the Unemployed, the Corporation shall start Municipal Farms and Market Gardens.

7.—Eight hours, or less, to be the normal working day for all Corporation employees, and the minimum wage to be 24s. per week.

8.—Depôts to be opened for the sale of Coal, or any commodity which the Corporation contracts for in bulk, at a price which will meet the cost of distribution.

9.—Abolition of Gas Meter Rents.

10.—All Corporation Employees to be placed on equal footing with regard to holidays, without loss of wages.

I am also opposed to Compulsory Vaccination, and would advocate in addition to the above, Municipal Bakeries, Medical Branch, Election of Magistrates, Abolition of Aldermen, Minimum Wage for Workmen and Maximum Wage for Officials, Publication of the Borough Accounts, and would advocate the right of Reporters attending Committee Meetings.

Faithfully yours,

THOMAS FREDERICK RICHARDS.

Central Committee Rooms, 3, Liverpool Street,
November 14th, 1894.

Martin Curley was ILP candidate for Latimer in 1894 and was secretary of the Labour Club.

Tom Carter was secretary of the Amalgamated Society of Engineers and a founding member of the ILP and the Leicester Co-operative Engineers' Society. He was president and secretary of the Trades Council.

The ILP's programme of outdoor meetings for the summer of 1895.

Jabez Chaplin was joint secretary of the Leicester Hosiery Union and left the Liberals to help found the local ILP. He had a resounding, clarion voice and it was said that no one ever complained that they could not hear him. According to one local paper 'his blend of rich humour in his practical, homely talks made him one of the most popular speakers'. He was soon elected to the town council.

Chaplin was not afraid of criticism and was a complete individualist in both his public and private life. When his wife died, he married her sister – something almost unknown then and seemed to many to be quite immoral. He was a Spiritualist and lived an extremely austere life – he neither smoked nor drank and had little interest in material possessions.

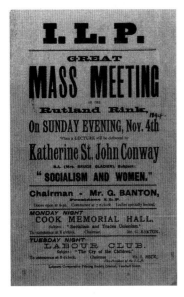

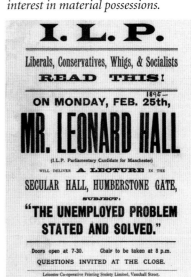

Above: 1895 bazaar advert. With no wealthy backers, the ILP was always short of money.
Right and left: Evening lectures given at the Secular Hall.

A Co-operative Commonwealth

During the 1890s there was a steady growth in co-operatively run factories. Some were promoted with the help of the trade unions and others grew from the workers themselves. By the early 20th century, Leicester had more co-operatively run factories than any other town in Britain and had become the national centre of the producers' co-operative movement. These co-partnership productive societies provided a range of goods that were sold through the co-op shops, and the ideal of co-operation found support with both the older generation of liberal trade unionists and the younger socialists. While the hope that these co-operatives could somehow replace capitalist production was utopian, Beatrice Webb's view that these enterprises were doomed to failure was somewhat premature.

The Glenfield 'Progress' producer Co-op was founded in 1892 with advice and help from Equity Shoes in Leicester. Its founder and manager, J.H. Brewin, was a Blaby Liberal councillor and Poor Law Guardian.

Mr. AMOS MANN,
President of the Leicester Co-operative Society.

Amos Mann, 1855–1939, was one of the founders of the Leicester Anchor Boot and Shoe Co-operative Productive Society, of which he was president for more than 20 years. Mann was one of Britain's leading advocates of producers' co-operation. Although he was elected as a Liberal councillor in 1897, his sympathies were always with Labour.

He was a lifelong abstainer and a speaker on temperance platforms. He was a member of Leicester No.1 branch of NUBSO and the Church of Christ. He was elected president of the Leicester Co-operative Society in 1908, being re-elected annually to the presidency until shortly before his death in 1939. Mann was outstanding among the pioneers of the Anchor Tenants Ltd, creators of the Humberstone Garden Suburb, being both a shareholder and a committee member. He lived there during the latter part of his life.

1915 advertisement.

Anchor: an offshoot of Equity

J.T. Taylor.

In 1892 J.T. Taylor, who was a member of the management committee of Equity Shoes, suggested the formation of a co-operative to produce children's footwear. This led to the formation of the Anchor Boot Society, whose early members, like Taylor himself, were drawn from the Church of Christ sect.

Taylor was originally president of the Anchor Society, but from January 1896 he became the manager of the factory, which had expanded into a new premises in Asfordby Street, North Evington. Anchor manufactured the 'Clef' brand of ladies' boots and shoes and the 'Fultred' brand for children.

Taylor was also treasurer of the ILP and played a prominent role in the formation of the Anchor Tenants Ltd, the co-op which was responsible for the development and building of the Humberstone Garden Suburb.

Advertisement, 1915.

The Anchor Boot and Shoe factory in Asfordby Street, North Evington, c.1903. This second factory was built by Arthur Wakerley and opened in April 1898.

PIGGY IN DANGER OF COMING TO PIECES.

The Trades Council was the co-ordinating body of the trade union movement in Leicester. In the late 1880s it wielded considerable political influence within the dominant Liberal Party. However, during the 1890s the Trades Council committed itself to independent Labour representation, initially standing candidates in its own name and then backing those from the ILP. The Trades Council then became the scene of battles between the newly arrived Socialists and the old Liberal unionists. However, it did not tear itself apart, as this cartoon from The Wyvern (October 1894) suggests, but instead gradually lost its power and status.

Alderman William Inskip JP, 1852–1899 (above) was a Lib-Lab trade unionist of the old school. He lacked formal education, but had read very widely. In 1886 he was elected general secretary of the Boot and Shoe Union and dominated the union for many years. He was contemptuous of egalitarianism and believed that social progress could be made through the generous rewarding of thrift and energy. He was elected to the council via the Trades Council and Liberal Association in 1891. He led the union during the 1895 lock-out, and when he died of TB aged 47 many Leicester firms closed for a few hours to allow workers to attend his funeral.

Presented Gratis with "THE WYVERN," May 25th, 1894.

RATHER MORE THAN HE CAN SWALLOW.

At the Edinburgh conference on Saturday, a political creed was formulated for the benefit of the Shoe Trade Parliamentary candidate: Alderman Inskip moved an amendment to the "Nationalisation of the means of production" clause, but it was not carried.

During the 1890s, Inskip came under increasing pressure from the Socialists in the union. He is shown above as a conjuror swallowing the Socialists' policies of Adult Suffrage, Old Age Pensions, Church Disestablishment, an Eight Hour Day, Graduated Income Tax and Triennial Parliaments. However, he finds the Nationalisation of the Means of Production too hard to swallow.

THE IMPENDING
LOCK-OUT
IN THE
BOOT & SHOE
TRADE.

A leaflet issued before the lock-out of 1895.

W.B. Hornidge, president and later general secretary of NUBSO between 1893–1908, despite chronic illness. He was a Liberal and Secularist.

The Great Lock-Out

On 13 March 1895, factory owners who were members of the Boot and Shoe Employers' Association shut their doors to their workers. Employees could only return to work if they signed a declaration not to join the union and not to help any union member financially. Nationally, about 46,000 workers were affected by the lock-out. In Leicester the press carried reports of demonstrations outside local factories against non-unionists. On 21 March a 'monstre' demonstration was called in Leicester and the *Leicester Daily Mercury* reported that: 'It was not possible to give an accurate estimate of the numbers participating, but an idea of it may be obtained from the fact that, walking for the most part four abreast it took the people just 50 minutes to pass a given point, so the procession would be about a mile in length…'

There were three bands in the procession, the Albion band at the head, a band made up entirely of shoe hands and the Wigston band. As the procession passed the shoe factories the bands changed from the usual military march tune into the *Dead March*, while the marchers engaged in what was described as 'lung exercise'. On passing the St Crispin Co-operative shoe works, which had been set up by the union and was working, the workers lined the windows and gave the marchers a 'lusty cheer'.

An effigy, clothed in a black coat with a 'tall' hat and wearing kid gloves, was borne by a couple of men and caused a good deal of merriment in the crowd. Presumably this was intended to be typical of boot manufacturers, for on the back was a card containing the words:

'Down with the wretch who turns out a scab, Down with the master who is all on the grab.'

William Inskip won public sympathy in his condemnation of the employers' rejection of arbitration. However, after nearly six weeks, with the union funds virtually exhausted, a settlement was reached. Although the employers did not succeed in eliminating the influence of the union, they obtained a free hand to introduce new machinery. The consequent technical revolution resulted in a considerable loss of craft jobs and an increase in the employment of young men and women.

Right: An anonymous handbill produced during the dispute designed to discourage workers from returning to work on the employers' terms. The press reported a number of demonstrations outside factories where non-unionists were working.

A handbill for the union's great demonstration.

A seminal moment in Leicester's Labour history as the 'monstre' demonstration of boot and shoe workers wends its way to the Belgrave Grounds on 21 March 1895, during the employers' lock-out. The banner refers to the employers' rejection of arbitration. (This photograph was previously thought to be of the 1905 Unemployment March.)

In 1894, local members of the defunct National Association of Builders' Labourers formed the Leicester and District Builders' Labourers Protective, Accident and Burial Society. In 1896 the association had 851 members in two branches and by 1898 membership exceeded 1,000. In 1907 it amalgamated with 25 other small local bodies to form the National Association of Builders' Labourers and this association in turn became the Altogether Builders' Labourers and Constructional Workers Society some time around 1920. This body merged with the Transport and General Workers Union in 1934.

It is likely that the banner was painted around 1900 by Tutills of London. The slogan on the banner had been used by local Chartists in 1838. The buildings in the circular panels are: the East Gates Coffee House at the top of Churchgate (bottom right), the Rutland pub on Wharf Street, the Castle Gateway and Mary de Castro. The central panel illustrates the benefits of union membership with depictions of the union providing health care (left) and Aesop's fable of the bundle of sticks that cannot be broken when they are bound together (above). Also illustrated are the Good Samaritan (above) and widows' benefits (left). The central panel shows an unidentified building under construction. The banner has been in Leicester Museum's store for many years.

The reverse of the banner. This shows the newly constructed Leicester School of Art (now the Hawthorne Building of De Montfort University).

Friendly Societies

In the years before the welfare state, working people used friendly societies to guard against bad times. On the left is the banner of the Thurmaston Friendly Society, founded in 1843, whose motto was 'Help In Times of Need.' The images on the banner are typical of 19th-century trade union iconography. The two figures seen by day and night presumably refer to the good and bad times while the lion lies down with the lamb (the strong helping the weak) with the aid of a cornucopia of plenty. The hands symbolise strength in unity, while the whole tableau is overseen by a masonic all-seeing eye. The other side of the banner carries the motto 'Amicitia, Amor et Veritas' (Friendship, Love and Truth).

The reverse of the Thurmaston Friendly Society banner, made by Tutills c.1900. It was recently discovered by the Thurmaston Heritage Group.

A common ash pit and pail closet side by side in Taylor Street. In 1872 the town council introduced pail closets in slum areas as a way of dealing with overflowing cesspools and an inadequate sewage system. The pails were regularly collected and the 'night soil' carted away by train. Taylor Street ran at right angles to where the railway line crosses Humberstone Road and led into Palmerstone Street. Tom Barclay described the inhabitants of the area as scissor-grinders, glaziers and 'mush-fakers', where women stitch gloves at starvation wages.

At the turn of the century, Leicester's poor lived in unsanitary slum housing. It was here that infant mortality was high and TB and diphtheria prevalent. The Winifred Street council flats (above), completed in 1900, were the council's first attempt to provide better housing for the poor. However, the high cost of the scheme caused by the Government's financial rules meant that the rents were beyond the reach of most poor families. It was only in 1919 that the town council began to build houses once again.

A gang of navvies pose with a missionary on a steam-powered crane, c.1897. This photograph shows the construction of the 'bowstring' girder bridge across Braunstone Gate. Navvies were still considered to be unruly, godless men who were seen by churchmen and Victorian moralists as ripe for conversion. To provide this guidance and instruction, missionaries served the navvy communities that accompanied the line's construction.

Navvies pause for a moment during the construction of a girder bridge at Duns Lane, Leicester, c.1897. The beneficial side effect of the construction of the Great Central Railway was the demolition of several streets of slum housing. In the background is the Braunstone Gate girder bridge.

Taken at a contractor's depot in around 1897, this photograph shows the blacksmith's shop in Mowmacre Hill, Leicester. Together with the huge numbers of men working with pick and shovel, many so-called navvies were actually skilled blacksmiths, steel erectors, bridge builders, miners, enginemen and brick layers.

The Braunstone Gate 'bowstring' Bridge – seen here under construction c.1897. The navvies involved with the construction lean against and pose around one of the side girders; 24 in total plus a dog. This bridge was built by the Wolverhampton firm Henry Lovatt.

Leicester Co-operative Society General Board, 1898. Top row: S. Kemp, A. Greatorex, J. Holden (manager), J.T. Mayes. Middle row: G. Gamble, F. Stacey, E.S. Yates, G. Bastard, S.C. Hubbard (cashier). Bottom row: A. Clayton, A. Mann, J. Pywell (treasurer), A. Lythall (president), H. Harriott (secretary), J.H. Woolley.

The High Street store after its extension in 1900.

The Co-operative Corn Mill on Ash Street was a commanding structure, standing five floors high. It was a great source of pride to the local Co-operative movement. Built to meet the needs of the expanding Co-operative movement in the 1870s, it went into voluntary liquidation before being run solely by the Leicester Society after 1888.

Thomas Hind (1838–1912) was the architect responsible for the Co-op's Central Stores on High Street, completed in 1884. He also designed the Victoria Model Lodging House on Britannia Street. He was a member of the LCS Board and a Liberal town councillor.

Above: The offices of the Leicester Co-operative Society on Union Street, designed by T.A. Hind, were opened in 1904 and cost £10,000 to build.

In 1900 the LCS bought a block of shops on High Street. This building had been Ye Old Crowne Inne. Although tempting offers were made to buy the licence from the Society, the temperance lobby on the Co-op Board ensured that these offers were refused and the shop shown above was opened. When the central store was extended in 1901, the drapery department was established on this site. The entrance to the Co-operative Hall is on the right of the picture.

Ramsay MacDonald and the Liberals

Ramsay MacDonald 1866–1937, can reasonably be considered one of the Labour Party's three major founding fathers. In 1899 he was successfully nominated as candidate for the two-member Leicester constituency by T.F. Richards. However, his vote in the 1900 General Election caused one of Liberal candidates to be defeated by the Tories.

In 1900, MacDonald became secretary of the newly-formed Labour Representation Committee and, in the years before the outbreak of World War One, he exercised a growing and visible influence over the growth of the young Labour Party. MacDonald was regarded sympathetically by the local Liberal political establishment and it was his personal relationship with the local factory owner Sir Edward Wood that provided the basis of Labour's electoral pact with the Liberals. This alliance ensured his election in 1906 and in Parliament he worked closely with the Liberals on such issues as Lloyd George's 'People's Budget' of 1909, the National Insurance Bill of 1911 and Irish Home Rule.

Ramsay MacDonald, c.1900.

Henry Broadhurst, c.1903, the Liberal MP for Leicester 1894–1909. He was an ex-trade unionist and was regarded as a 'working man' MP.

Alderman Sir Edward Wood (c.1903) helped broker the Lib-Lab pact.

F.J. Gould

F.J. Gould was the Secular Society's organiser. In 1900 he stood as the Society's candidate for the School Board and was elected. He then successfully persuaded the board to institute a programme of secular moral education. He also helped re-establish Barclay's *Leicester Pioneer* as a paper of 'social progress' and contributed numerous articles and reports. After joining the ILP, he acted as secretary to the 15 Labour councillors. In 1904 he was elected to the town council in his own right.

Left: F.J. Gould's election address, 1900.

PIONEER PAMPHLETS, No. 1.

Reprinted from "THE LEICESTER PIONEER"

Above: The cover of an anti-war pamphlet, c.1900. The ILP was opposed to the Boer War.

Right: This photograph is thought to be of ILP members, c.1901. Some of the group are wearing the ILP badge of a woollen shamrock-shaped flower, with each leaf being a different colour. White was for purity or absence of crime, green for nature or return to the land and red for universal brotherhood.

Below: A group of Secularists on an outing. William Warner (son of one of the founders of the Socialist League) is sat in the front holding a copy of the Socialist newspaper The Clarion. *It might be possible that these were members of the Secular Cycling Club that was affiliated to the Clarion movement.*

The Shoe Trade Hall

The Shoe Trade Hall in St James Street (right) was completed in 1903 at a cost of £6,000. It was built for the NUBSO No.1 Branch by Leicester Builders' Co-operative Society.

The building comprised offices for the presidents, vice-presidents and secretaries of the two Leicester branches, while the whole of the second floor was given over to the National Union. A large assembly hall (bottom right), capable of holding 600–700 people, was immediately behind the ground-floor offices.

Charles Freake (1847–1910)

Charlie Freake became general president of NUBSO in 1899. He had allied himself with Socialists in the union and had previously been a member of the London County Council. In 1904, he was elected to the town council for St Margaret's ward.

Freake was a man of tough fibre, resilient and sanguine. In appearance he was typical of the 'respectable' Victorian trade union leader, with his beard, stained with snuff and beer, and the long frock coat that he was still wearing in the first decade of the 20th century. 'A man of dignified presence and considerable personal magnetism…with a certain brusqueness of manner…not cultured or polished rhetorician, but his rugged eloquence often made greater impression than any refined oratory could have done.' – *Leicester Daily Post*, 1910.

Leicester No.1 Branch Executive of the National Union of Boot and Shoe Operatives, c.1903. Left to right: T. Orton (vice-president), T.F. Richards (president), H. Williams (standing), Richard Croft (secretary), M. Parker (standing), Harry Hardwick Woolley.

Leicester No.2 Branch Executive of the National Union of Boot and Shoe Operatives (clickers and pressmen), c.1903. Back row, left to right: R. Harris, A.J. Wilson, J. Day, E. Whatton. Front row: W. Lowe (vice-president), Alf Hill (president), W. Wilks.

The Labour Representation Committee

LRC secretary: Cllr G.E. Hubbard.

The Leicester Labour Representation Committee was formed in March 1903 and it was only in 1906 that it became officially known as the Labour Party. It was a delegate body representing affiliated organisations with no individual membership. George Hubbard was its first secretary and Tom Curley (from the National Union of Boot and Shoe Operatives) its first president. During 1903, the LRC, together with the ILP, moved into the Trades Council Hall. The LRC took over the important functions of coordinating, financing and superintending elections. In 1906 George Hubbard became Ramsay MacDonald's election agent and it was claimed that the success of the LRC in Leicester was largely due to his organising ability.

When, in September 1903, the *Leicester Pioneer* had got into financial difficulties, it was bailed out by LRC supporters. It appeared in January 1904 as 'The Official Organ of the Labour Representation Committee'. George Hubbard was one of those who guaranteed the expenses of the first three numbers out of his own pocket and he became secretary of the new company. The *Pioneer* continued to be published until 1929.

The Trades Council outside the newly-built Trades Hall in 1903.

'The Finest Boot Factory In The Kingdom'

By 1890 1,300 workers were employed by the CWS at its Duns Lane factory and demand for its footwear continued to grow. A four-acre site in the rural surroundings at Knighton Fields was bought for a new factory and all the building work and design was carried out by the CWS.

It was hailed as 'the finest boot factory in the kingdom' and it certainly was the largest, since its main room covered an acre and a half. When the Wheatsheaf Works opened on 4 November 1891 the Leicester Co-op provided a meat tea for 1,300 guests at one sitting. At the time, it was the largest tea party ever held in Leicester. The factory was able to make 50,000 pairs of shoes in a week.

The CWS Wheatsheaf Boot and Shoe Works, Knighton Fields, c.1915.

An interior view of the CWS giant Wheatsheaf factory, c.1913. At its height of production, 2,200 people worked here.

The machinists' room at the CWS Wheatsheaf factory, c.1913.

The Wheatsheaf Works c.1898, before the addition of the clock tower.

View of the Clicking Department, c.1898.

View of one portion of the lasting room, c.1898.

View of the finishing room, c.1898.

Leicester Builders Ltd was formed in 1896. By the end of the century it had built houses in the Western Road extension and in Oakley and Humberstone roads. It also worked as a jobbing builder for other Co-operative enterprises. In 1903 it completed the prestigious Shoe Trade Hall for the Boot and Shoe Union.

The committee of the Leicester Co-operative Printing Society, c.1898. John Potter, a founder of Equity, is in the centre of the picture.

The Leicester Co-operative Engineers was founded in 1894 by members of the local branch of the Amalgamated Society of Engineers. Its first work of importance was to help move the engine and machinery of the Equity Boot and Shoe Society to its new factory in Western Road. Among its founders was Tom Carter, a prominent member of the ILP.

The offices of the Leicester Co-operative Printing Society Ltd at 99 Churchgate in the early 1900s.

Leicester Co-operative Printers: Printers to the Labour Movement

Leicester Co-operative Printers was founded in 1892 and was helped into existence by the other locally established Co-operatives. From letterpress printing, the society expanded into bookbinding and later into cardboard boxes. It established branches in London and Kettering. The society was managed by a board elected by shareholders and employees.

Frederick Sutton, 1854–1932 (left), was secretary of the Leicester Typographical Society. He was the Trades Council's secretary from 1910–12 and was a pioneer of the Leicester Co-operative Printing Society. He was later a Labour town councillor for Abbey ward (1909–20).

CO-OPERATIVE PRINTING SOCIETY,

IN SUPPORT OF THE ABOVE OBJECT, A

PUBLIC MEETING

WILL BE HELD IN THE

CO-OPERATIVE HALL,

HIGH STREET, LEICESTER.

ON SATURDAY, MAY 7, 1892.

CHAIR TO BE TAKEN AT 8 O'CLOCK

A notice of the founding meeting.

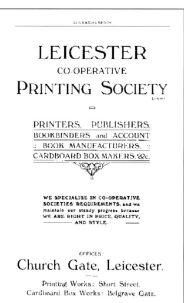

57

Monotype keyboard operators in May 1913 at Leicester Co-operative Printers. The Monotype composition system, in use since just before 1900, produced individual types composed and spaced, ready to print. The keyboard operator's keystrokes were recorded as holes along a roll of paper tape. This information was then read by a caster that made the letters.

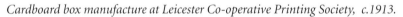

Cardboard box manufacture at Leicester Co-operative Printing Society, c.1913.

The Sperope Boot Manufacturers in Barwell, c.1900. This was registered as a Co-op in 1891 and made ladies' and children's boots and shoes with the trademark Sperope.

Co-partnership Co-operatives

The premises of the Leicester 'Self-Help' Boot and Shoe Manufacturing Society Ltd, Dartford Road. The 'Self Help' Society grew out of the St Crispin Co-op, which was started by trade unionists who could find no work following the 1895 lock-out. Although the society initially made a loss, the Boot and Shoe Union bought shares and the society eventually prospered. It was still in business until after 1945.

The Morning Star Sundries Society packed products into boxes for other Co-operatives. It started out in 1903 and in 1908 moved to a factory in Aylestone Road.

The Excelsior Boot and Shoe Manufacturing Society begun in Sileby in 1906. During the 1920s, a new factory was built to replace the one shown.

The March to London

On 5 June 1905 around 450 men set out to march to London to protest over unemployment and the treatment of the unemployed by the Poor Law. The previous month striking shoemakers from Northamptonshire had also marched to London, but this was the first protest of its kind by the unemployed. It was the culmination of months of local agitation led by the secretary of the unemployed committee, George ('Sticky') White and Amos Sherriff, who was a Poor Law Guardian. Seven hundred had volunteered for the march, but just over half that number were chosen as fit enough for the venture. At the last minute the march was joined by the Revd F.L. Donaldson of St Mark's Church.

Although Sherriff and White were members of the ILP, there was not unanimous support for the march from the local Labour movement. The Trades Council voted 31–22 against supporting the march and only loaned the men its collecting boxes after the fiercest of discussions. Some, like George Banton, privately thought the venture was too huge an undertaking and might end in disaster, while those of the old school of trade unionism were not keen on street protests and extra-parliamentary action.

However, by the time the march set off it had captured the public imagination and an estimated 30,000 people turned out to give them a tumultuous farewell. Spruced up for the departure, wearing medals, and carrying water bottles and blankets, led by a banner and several bands, they moved off from the packed streets to the hymn tune of *Lead Kindly Light*.

The journey was no outing: funds were small, the men had been underfed for months and few had boots that could stand the miles of footslogging. They arrived in Market Harborough with what a local reporter described as 'poverty-stricken pomp' to a supper of a 1lb loaf, 2oz cheese and a cup of cocoa per man. They washed in cattle troughs filled with fresh water and slept in the cattle sheds on fresh hay. The journey continued in persistent and soaking rain and by the time they reached

Above: The marchers' three leaders: Amos Sherriff, Revd F.L. Donaldson (later known as the vicar of the unemployed) and George 'Sticky' White in London on Hampstead Heath.

Below: One of the badges worn by the marchers.

Northampton there was an urgent appeal for boots.

At Yardley, the local Co-op provided sacks for overcoats, knives being in great demand for cutting the armholes. On 8 June at Wildchanystead, a local publican was so moved by the plight of one poor fellow that he took off his own boots in the street and gave them to him. Two more days of chilling winds and driving rain saw the marchers in St Albans, breakfast being bread, butter and tea. By now the men had received a telegram from the Secretary of State for Home Affairs, giving news of the King's refusal to meet them.

On 10 June, the ragged army of 430 men reached London. They spent their first night in a Salvation Army shelter and were given the luxury of a meat tea by the ILP. They were welcomed in London at a mass meeting in Hyde Park in support of the Unemployed Bill, but more bad weather washed out the planned 'great rally'. The following day they attended a rally in Trafalgar Square, which was addressed by Leicester Labour leaders who had travelled down by train. Jabez Chaplin (who had originally opposed the march) told the crowd that: 'The men had not lost their work through drunkenness, carelessness or dishonesty, but because of the rapid introduction of new machinery.'

On Whit Monday the weather brightened and so did the men. They marched cheerfully to Parliament Hill Fields, four abreast, a chair was brought from a tea house at the foot of the hill to serve as a platform and the local leaders, supported by Ramsey McDonald for the ILP, addressed a crowd of more than 6,000 holidaymakers. Keir Hardie sent a telegram to Sherriff which read: 'Tell the men not to starve in silence, but keep agitating all the time. Nothing else avails until Socialism comes.'

To cheers for London, the ILP and the police, the men struck off across the heath towards Watford and the road home. It was an equally arduous journey and they arrived back on Saturday 18 June to a rapturous reception. Folwells pork butchers met the marchers outside Leicester with a cart load of pork pies and in the town they were greeted by a massive crowd, estimated to be 80,000.

The pictures above and below are taken from hand-coloured lantern slides. Above: A huge crowd, estimated at 30,000 people, turned out to send the marchers off from the Market Place. Below: An early morning wash in the cattle troughs at Market Harborough. One local businessman gave 400 tablets of soap for the long trek to London.

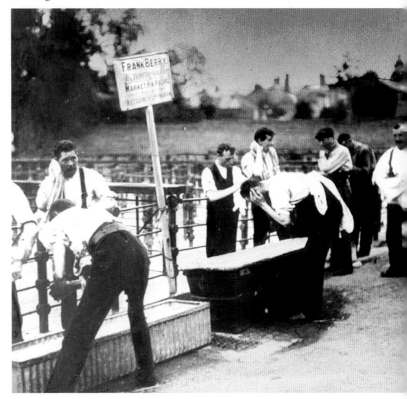

The march outside the London Road railway station.

The march passing the tram terminus on London Road.

Tuesday 13 June 1905: the marchers inside the Drill Hall at Watford on the return journey. Amos Sherriff is standing at the back.

Wednesday 7 June: picking up the wounded at Barton Cutting near Luton.

Wednesday 7 June: helping a comrade. Poor footwear was the cause of most of the casualties.

Members of the marchers' band had pawned their instruments and Amos Sherriff launched an appeal for money to get them redeemed. Mr Alfred Keightley (big drum), Mr Haynes (trombone) and an unknown euphonium and trumpet player are pictured after tea at Wellingborough on the return journey, Thursday 15 June 1905.

Amos Sherriff, Revd F.L. Donaldson and George White with other marchers at Wellingborough.

An advance guard of the marchers poses for a photograph in London near the Coffee Hut on Edgware Road. They are holding the Trades Council's precious collecting boxes. Sergeant Baxter, the one-legged war veteran, stands with his bicycle next to George White.

Councillor George Banton presents medals to the 416 marchers who made it back to Leicester. This ceremony took place outside Oadby shortly before the marchers' triumphant entry into the town. It is not known precisely how many had set out from Leicester, but 437 marchers reached London. Along the way, some dropped out and 16 found work. Alice Hawkins, whose husband Alf helped organise the march, is in the centre of the picture.

Sunday 18 June 1905: the exhausted marchers return to the Market Place.

The huge crowd watches as the marchers enter the Corn Exchange.

The Marchers' Return

'The bells were chiming three when the crowd in the Market Place caught the first throb of the drums. Patience and order gave way to excitement and disorder. The great mass of people heaved and swayed like corn before the wind. For a moment or two the police stood firm…No sooner did the thin line of marchers come into view than the crowd surged upon them. The leaders got through, but the rank and file were twisted and turned like a ribbon in the breeze. Women fainted and dropped, and were with great difficulty picked up and brought safely through. The police were helpless; they did all it was possible for them to do in the circumstances…

Suddenly, from the top of the Exchange steps, came an arresting figure: the Rev. F.L. Donaldson. Surpliced, and with hand uplifted, he asked for quiet. "Let us sing" he said, and immediately the band played the music of the beautiful hymn, *Lead Kindly Light*. The effect was magical. The crowd steadied itself, and wholeheartedly sang the words. The danger was passed.'

Leicester Daily Mercury.

Alice Hawkins, George White, Amos Sherriff, George Banton, Ramsay MacDonald, Frederic and Louise Donaldson are among many on the steps outside the Corn Exchange in the Market Place at the end of the great demonstration. From donations, each marcher received a medal, 3lb of beef, 3lb of potatoes, 1lb of sugar, ¼lb tea and three loaves plus 4s 6d in money.

A souvenir napkin printed in London in honour of the marchers. Many of the marchers had fought in the Boer War and the reference in the picture is to the use of imported Chinese workers in South Africa.

Equity Road and Humberstone Garden Suburb

At the turn of the century, there was little decent housing available for working people. Forty-five workers at the Anchor Shoe Co-operative took matters into their own hands and subscribed to their own co-operative housing venture. At Equity several building societies had been formed among the workers and 60 houses were built. In 1907, the Anchor tenants bought 48 acres of land at Humberstone for £48,000 and in a year had built a pair of cottages on Keyham Lane, which were let at 6s 3d per week. At that time there were 81 members of the co-partnership scheme.

The initial layout of Humberstone Garden Suburb was undertaken by the leading advocate of the garden city movement, Raymond Unwin. His design did not include a front parlour though, so a local man, George Hern, was employed by the tenants as their architect. By 1915 a total of 94 houses had been built, on streets such as Lilac and Chestnut avenues, Laburnum Road, Fern Rise and Keyham Lane, along with tennis courts, shops and a meeting house.

The Humberstone Garden Suburb is unique, not just because it predates both Letchworth and Hampstead, or because its original structure is still intact, but because it is the only garden suburb ever to be built by the members of a workers' Co-operative.

A completion ceremony in 1911.

Lilac Avenue, c.1915.

Houses on Keyham Lane, c.1915.

Houses on Keyham Lane, Humberstone, c.1915.

Left: An Equity worker stands proudly in front of his house, c.1898. The houses cost about £400 to build and contained four bedrooms, a bathroom, parlour, dining room, kitchen and scullery. Although Equity did not adopt the garden suburb model of design, these houses were of a far higher quality than ordinary working-class housing. As a result, Equity Road, off Narborough Road, was named 'in honour' of the works. Meanwhile, poorer workers continued to live in the slums in the centre of town.

Members of the Anchor Tenants' Building Department in 1909. On the left is the architect George Hern and on the far right is Sam Wilford. Others in the picture are Fat Dan, Mr Taylor, R. Law, W. Pawley, A. Wilford and Mr Darby. Their motto: 'not greater wealth, but simpler pleasures'.

The tennis courts at the Humberstone Garden Suburb in 1914. These were the first semi-detached houses built for working people in Leicester. This, rather than the tenement-style dwellings of Winifred Street, was the model for post-war council housing.

'Loaded up – Ramsay MacDonald M.P. will have a strenuous autumn this year. In addition to his ordinary work he is engaged to deliver some sixty addresses in all parts of the kingdom. There are not many porters who have to labour half as hard as this.' (Leicester Pioneer, 1907)

Ramsay MacDonald addressing a crowd somewhere in Leicester. He is accompanied by George Banton.

The cartoon on the left was originally published under the title 'The Slammed Door.' It was reused on N.C. Perkins's election address of 1909.

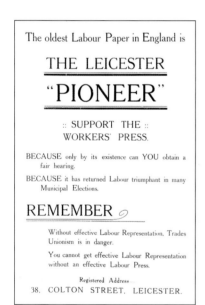

From 1907, the Leicester Pioneer's *cartoonist 'Bertwal' produced a string of political cartoons on local Labour themes. 'What Will It Say?' portrayed a Liberal councillor who had never spoken in the council chamber as the Sphinx. 'Better Starvation Than State Aid' attacks the failure of the council to introduce meals for poor children. Despite MacDonald's alliance with the Liberals, Liberalism was now being described by the local ILP as a manufacturers' doctrine unable to provide a humane solution to the problem of poverty and unemployment.*

'In Sinful Slumber'

Will nothing short of a brick through the window waken her?

In the 1900s, poverty and unemployment were the issues that distinguished Labour from the Liberals. Labour wanted 'relief without pauperisation', and berated the Liberals for handing out big pay increases to senior council officials. 'Parsimonious Prodigals' was the title of the Pioneer cartoon (below) from 1907.

COUNC. W. E. HINCKS ⎫ We don't care how thirsty you are. ⎫ ALD ROYCE (Chairman of Watch Committee) ⎫ Hooray! Exactly
AND   ⎬ In the interests of true economy, we   COUNC. FLINT (Chairman of Tram Committee) ⎬ what we think.
DR. BENNETT.   ⎭ *must* keep you away from the barrel. COUNC. JENNINGS (Chairman of Gas Committee) ⎭

This cartoon from 1908 shows Aldermen Vincent, a Tory, and George Banton carting off the 'Grand Old Liberal Party' to the museum. The Liberal Party is depicted as an old beadle (a parish officer with powers to punish misdemeanours) who has gone to sleep in his box. As a result of the Lib-Lab pact, such attacks on the Liberals soon became anathema in some Labour circles.

George Banton: Labour's Local Leader

It was George Banton's spadework that established the Independent Labour Party in Leicester. Although a carpenter by trade, in the 1890s he went into business as a coal merchant because no employer would want to give a job to a Labour councillor. By the early 1900s he led a 15-strong group of councillors.

He had known hardship and unemployment. At the age of 21 he had tramped from Leicester to Birmingham and then on to London in search of work. He stayed in London for several months then walked back to Birmingham and on to Liverpool.

He visited practically all the principal towns in Lancashire and Yorkshire looking for work and then he tramped back through Sheffield, Derby and Nottingham to settle in Leicester.

In 1913 he was adopted as the ILP candidate for the parliamentary bye-election of that year. Since his candidacy would have breached the electoral pact with the Liberals, Labour's national leadership forced him to withdraw.

George Banton was a carpenter by trade. Despite his opposition to World War One, he was twice elected to Parliament and became mayor in 1926.

Suffragists and Suffragettes

In the late 1900s, local women campaigning for the vote became divided over tactics. Younger women, tired of the worthiness of the older Suffrage Society, joined the more militant Women's Social and Political Union (Suffragettes) that became established in Leicester in 1907.

During the 1890s, the National Union of Women Workers formed a local branch, as did the Co-operative Women's Guild. Like the Railway Women's Guild (an offshoot of the Amalgamated Society of Railway Servants) it attracted working-class women.

In 1906 the Women's Labour League was founded in Leicester with Margaret MacDonald as its president. The league was organised exclusively for and by women and was affiliated to the Labour Party. It was active on women's suffrage and union organisation of women but it did not take any 'militant' action.

Marina Peach holding her eldest child, Margaret, in 1900. She was an ILP member and campaigned for a women's maternity hospital. She died in 1913, aged 40, after giving birth to her seventh child. At the time of her death she was president of the Women's Labour League. Her memorial was an 'Infant Consultation Centre' designed to promote 'Mothercraft'. It was opened in Highcross Street, which was then an area of high infant mortality.

Annie Stretton was a founder of the Women's Labour League, a Labour guardian and active in the Railway Women's Guild.

Ruth Banton, a Labour guardian and a founder of the Women's Labour League.

Mrs C. Willson was active in the Co-operative Women's Guild, a Labour guardian who campaigned for nursery and maternity provision.

Burton]   [Leicester.

LEICESTER WOMEN'S CO-OPERATIVE GUILD COMMITTEE.

Standing : Miss C. Woolley, Mrs. Osborne, Mrs. Willson, Mrs. Miles, Mrs. Turner (Sectional Council), Mrs. Ward, Mrs. Cox, Mrs. Matthews, Mrs. Baker.
Seated : Mrs. Wortley, Mrs. Widdowson, Mrs. Pywell (President), Mrs. Leadbeater (Secretary), Mrs. Kelly (Vice-President).

The Co-operative Women's Guild Committee in 1915. The Guild was started at a tea meeting held at the Oxford Street Chapel Sunday School in November 1890. During World War One, the guild was instrumental in establishing day nurseries for working mothers with children. By the mid-1920s there were 19 branches of the guild in Leicestershire.

Designed to ease the life of women at home and end the disturbance of the weekly wash, the Co-operative steam laundry was opened in 1910 on the corner of Ash and Larch Street. The society was proud that its employees worked in such good conditions with 'excellent sanitary provision' and a mess room for meals. In 1923, the laundry paid its workers 25 per cent above the level fixed by the Board of Trade with two weeks holiday with pay and two weeks' sick pay after two years. The laundry business grew and by the late 1920s no new customers could be taken on.

'Skiving' or thinning off the edges of the different parts of the shoe, ready for the fitters and machinists at the Equity factory in 1907, by Sylvia Pankhurst. The woman in the painting is thought to be the local suffragette Alice Hawkins (see page 90).

Sylvia Pankhurst: Artist, Suffragette and Socialist

The feminist and Socialist Sylvia Pankhurst (1882–1960) was an accomplished artist and designer. She produced the logo, scarves, brooches and publicity for the Women's Social and Political Union and its paper *Votes for Women*. In 1907 she made a tour, speaking at meetings and painting women at work and at home.

In Leicester, she spoke in the Market Place for the ILP and at meetings of the suffragettes. She thought the work that the women did in the Equity factory was monotonous and was surprised to hear them say of her painting 'I would never have the patience for that.'

While in prison between 1913 and 1914, Sylvia endured 10 hunger strikes, but her experience of ordinary women's life during her tour led her to question the WSPU's tactics of increased militancy, stone throwing and hunger strikes.

Untitled Gouache *by Sylvia Pankhurst, painted in 1907 at the Equity Boot and Shoe factory.*

The Murals

Revd F.L. Donaldson (1860–1953) became vicar of St Mark's Church, Leicester, in 1896. In 1910 he initiated and supervised the painting of the sanctuary murals – seven large canvas panels painted in oils by James Eadie-Read depicting Christ as the 'Apotheosis of Labour.'

James Eadie-Reid (1856–1926) was born in Dundee and studied at Edinburgh. He was a friend of the Pre-Raphaelite Brotherhood and was a painter specialising in stained-glass windows and murals for churches on religious themes. He exhibited at the Royal Scottish Academy and the London Salon.

In a pamphlet describing the murals, Donaldson wrote: 'The Church of St Mark's stands in a town of 244,255 souls, of whom the greater number belong to what are termed "the working classes." St Mark's is one of the chief working-class parishes of the town, and contains towards 15,000 souls. In this parish there is represented much of the tragedy and pathos, shame and horror of modern social conditions – infant mortality, child labour, underpayment or sweating of men and women, decadence of physical life, consumption and premature death.'

The poverty, pain and sorrow he had encountered among his parishioners is depicted in the two outermost panels: 'Labour suffers under Tyranny and Oppression, while Mammon, with money bags on his lap, is waited on by Luxury and watched over by the Angel of Sorrow.'

To the extreme left is seen a man in middle life, healthy and well, but outcast from society. 'He holds his coat in his hands and sees no hope. This figure represents the great problem of the Unemployed, for whom society has no place. Another, broken and bandaged, represents the mutilation of thousands in modern industry.'

'A dim figure nearby symbolises Society, cold, hard and indifferent in the midst of the tragedy of life. As the panels progress, men and women begin to assist one another with the help of good leadership from priests, labour leaders, thinkers or social workers, until finally the competitive system is replaced by one of social ownership and Co-operation.'

After standing empty for 20 years, St Mark's Church, which is a Grade II listed building, has now been renovated and is in use for private functions. The paintings have yet to be restored.

Rev. F. L. DONALDSON,
Chaplain to the Leicester Unemployed March.
Photo. taken at Bedford Chapel, London, on Whit-Monday, June 12th, 1905, prior to the start for home.

Donaldson in London in 1905 outside the Bedford Chapel, where the unemployed marchers stayed. In 1913 he returned to London leading a deputation of Church of England clergy to the Prime Minister, Asquith, on the subject of women's suffrage.

Below: The inside of the church showing the murals, c.1911.

Detail of first right panel.

Detail of second left panel.

Detail of first left panel.

Detail of second right panel.

The Labour Party conference held in Leicester at the Temperance Hall in February 1911. J.R. Clynes is on his feet, flanked by Keir Hardie to his left and Ramsay MacDonald beside the lady to his right. The Revd F.L. Donaldson sits behind MacDonald's left shoulder.

W.H. Lowe (hosiery) George Green (railwaymen) and George Sedgwick (boot and shoe) were all prominent Liberal trade unionists. Since Labour and the Liberals had an electoral pact, it is not so surprising that this is an illustration from the 1911 Labour Party conference souvenir.

Above: the Town Council Labour Group, October 1910. Back row, left to right: J.K. Kelly, H. Hand, J.W. Murby, A.H. Reynolds, F. Sutton, N.C. Perkins. Front row: F.F. Riley, A. Hill, J. Chaplin, G. Banton, G.E. Hubbard, G.A. Kenney, A. Sherriff.

Below: Labour members of the Board of Guardians in 1910 (responsible for administering the workhouse). Back row, left to right: M.T. Parker, E.H. Pinchbeck, A. Martin, Revd C.S. Smith, J. Ball, J.L. Harrison. Front row: D. McCarthy, W.J. Moore, Miss M.J. Bell, W. Taylor, J.S. Salt, C. Harris.

In 1901 Mary Bell became the first Labour woman to be elected to the Board of Guardians. However, she was best known as an official of the women's branch of NUBSO. She was elected to the union's National Council and remained a champion of working women throughout her union career. She sought to commit the union to equal pay for women and unsuccessfully tried to get women to be allowed to work in all departments of the boot and shoe trade at the man's rate. In 1916 she married Freddy Richards and was thereafter known as Mrs Bell-Richards.

Non-union labour, employed at lower rates outside the union strongholds of Leicester and Northampton, was a constant threat to living standards of Leicester shoe workers. At the time of this leaflet, the women's branch of the union, under its militant Suffragette leadership, had just broken away from NUBSO to form the National Independent Union of Women Boot and Shoe Workers. This new union survived until the 1930s.

In 1910, NUBSO promoted T.F. Richard's idea of a 'union stamp'. The hope was that consumer power could be used to increase the sale of footwear made by workers paid at trade union rates. This fair trade idea was adopted by many of the Producer Co-operatives, but it did not have the success that the union had hoped for in the private sector.

In 1906 Cllr T.F. Richards became MP for Wolverhampton West. After his defeat in 1910 he became president of NUBSO. With spats and bow ties, he was counted as one of the first dandies of the trade union movement.

The London Road station during the 1911 rail strike. On Winston Churchill's orders, troops were sent to guard stations all over the country. However, this massive show of force did not break the strike and the employers were forced to concede.

Troops on the Leicester goods yard signal box in August 1911.

An undated photograph of members of the Amalgamated Society of Railway Servants. The banner is typical of the 'widow and orphan' scene that adorned many railwaymen's banners. The Society was formed in 1872 and, following a merger in 1913, became the National Union of Railwaymen.

John Murby (born c.1872) worked at the CWS Wheatsheaf factory before joining the Self Help Boot and Shoe Co-op, where he became a member of the committee. He was an active Wesleyan and the Pioneer described him as being 'powerfully religious, but Socialism adorns his religion…Like so many Socialist speakers, his oratorical skills have been forged on the anvil of necessity. If you survive, no audience has terrors for you. Murby survived'. In 1909 he was elected as a town councillor for Castle ward. He was chairman of the Leicester ILP in 1913–16 and a member of its national executive.

Who? Who? Who?

Who had the Miners shot at **Featherstone** in 1893?
THE LIBERALS !

Who had the workers shot at **Belfast** in 1908?
THE LIBERALS !

Who had the miners of **Tonypandy** bludgeoned?
THE LIBERALS !

Who shot the workers at **Llanelly** ?
THE LIBERALS !

WHO BROUGHT THE SOLDIERS to Leicester and would have fired on the Workers?
The Liberals.

Who is a Food Taxer?
HEWART, the Liberal !

Who would be a Food Taxer?
WILSHERE, the Tory !

Who supports the unjust and fraudulent Insurance Act?
HEWART, the Liberal !

Who also supports the Insurance Fraud?
WILSHERE, the Tory !

Who would sweep ALL Food Taxes and Insurance Frauds away?

Hartley
THE SOCIALIST.

An advert for E.R. Hartley, the British Socialist Party candidate in the 1913 bye-election. He hastily stood when MacDonald and the national Labour leadership barred the Leicester ILP from putting forward George Banton because of the Lib-Lab pact.

Russian Tyranny in a Leicester Factory
Victimised for Trade Unionism

Owing to the Local Press, with the exception of the "*Leicester Pioneer,*" refusing to publish our letter, we are compelled in the interest of trade unionists to resort to this means of bringing our case before the general public.

"Sir,

In these days of Osborne judgements, and when public men of all shades of opinion are glorifying trade unions, may we show what may be done to trade unionists in Leicester simply because they are trade unionists? We hear of tyranny being practised everywhere, and are called upon to resent and overthrow it. Trade unions are looked upon as the chosen instrument to overthrow the tyrant.

We have worked for a large hosiery mill in Leicester as winders, four years and two years respectively. A fortnight ago the firm endeavoured to reduce the price of work, which meant a reduction of 3/- to 4/- per week. We ceased work for about two hours, and eventually were told to resume work on the old conditions. The girls decided to join the Hosiery Union on the following Saturday, so that we should have someone to fight for us in time of trouble, but when Saturday came the usual excuse was made—they were afraid to join for fear of being discharged. So only my sister and myself joined. We met the officials, and it was arranged to call a meeting of the whole of the girls for organising purposes, and a letter from our officials to that effect was sent round the firm. When leaving work that night to attend the meeting the word went round that those who went had better look out. Consequently only three of us turned up. The following morning the forewoman of our department went round to the majority of the girls and enquired who had attended the meeting. Last Friday we and the other one who had attended the meeting received a week's notice in writing. We were instructed to inquire of the manager as to the cause of our dismissal. We asked if it was bad workmanship,

and we were told that our work and characters were everything that could be desired. When further questioned as to whether the trade meeting we attended had anything to do with it, the manager candidly confessed it had, and he said had we not attended the meeting all would have been well. When we further questioned him as to our rights to attend any meeting after our day's work was over, he admitted we had a perfect right to go where we liked. But, he replied emphatically, on the other hand he too, had a perfect right to dismiss and set on whom he chose, so we are ruthlessly dismissed, our bread snatched from our mouths. Please note the firm are on overtime and also advertising for hands. We appealed to the union we joined, but they are powerless, as the firm absolutely refused to see our officials over our discharge, so bitter are they against trade unionism.

Ought we to endure such tyrannny in silence? We think not. We frankly admit we are only young recruits to the ranks of the trade unionists. But if each unit of us are to be checked in like manner and no protest made, how can we expect to strengthen our ranks further in the interests of the thousands of our sisters working in the trade. We therefore humbly and respectfully ask you in the great cause of freedom and liberty of the subject, to give our experience publicity, as our statements are truthful and ungarbled.

We are, yours very respectfully,

NELLIE WHITE, Age 19 years,
IVY WHITE, Age 16 years.

63, All Saints' Road, Leicester."

A MEETING will be held in the Market Place,
On SUNDAY MORNING NEXT, October 30th, at 11 prompt,
to protest against the dismissal of two girls for joining the Trade Union.

Chair to be taken by MR. F. BURTON, President of Leicester Trades Council.

Speakers:
Ald. J. CHAPLIN, J.P. (Secretary of Hosiery Union).   Ald. GEO. BANTON, J.P.
Coun. F. SUTTON (Secretary Leicester Trades Council).
Mr. THOS. ORTON (President No 1. Branch Boot & Shoe Operatives).
Coun. H. HAND (Carpenters & Joiners' Union).
Coun. G. A. KENNEY (President of Trimmers' Union).   Coun. A. SHERRIFF.
Miss L. WILSON (Secretary No. 3 Branch Boot & Shoe Union).

Above: A strike picket of women workers outside Thomas Brown & Company's ladies' shoe factory in Humberstone Road, Leicester, c.1912.

Above: F. Burton, president of the Trades Council for 1910, a delegate from the Trimmers' Society.

Left: A leaflet issued by the Leicester Hosiery Union in 1910. The victimised workers, Ivy and Nellie White, were the daughters of George White, one of the leaders of the 1905 Unemployed March.

Above: A suffrage procession outside London Road station in 1910. Eva Lines and Violet West are seated left and right.

Below: The front of the parade, led by a brass band.

The Suffragettes

In 1907, Mrs Pankhurst's Women's Social and Political Union established a branch in Leicester. The following is an account of a WSPU meeting.

'An enormous concourse gathered in the Market Place on Monday evening to agree or differ with two suffragettes who for an hour held the fort heroically. The watch committee decided not only to protect the speakers, but to preserve order in the crowd. (In the crowd of 500 people was the chair of the watch committee Cllr W.E. Hincks.) This decision had a very salutary effect on the hooligans who had been baiting the Suffragettes in the most cowardly manner on the two previous Thursdays; the actions of the magistrates in fining two of the ruffians heavily was beneficial. But what conduced a magnificent and peaceable meeting was the spirit of the noble martyr MISS EMILY W DAVISON which was ever present…

Miss Wyatt of Leicester, the chairwoman, opened the meeting at 6pm and appealed for fair play. Although the hour was teatime the crowd grew rapidly and Supt. Carson arranged his men, uniformed and otherwise, at close intervals throughout the crowd. Then Miss E. Grew was called to speak. Erect in pose, strong in physique, cultured in style, bold in delivery, courteous and defiant in manner, fluent of speech and with eyes flashing, she poured out an avalanche of rhetoric upon friend and foe alike. It was an inspiring scene – that great crowd listening to the courageous girl in the close fitting black costume with the little green knitted pork pie cap…

Miss Grew put her case amid cheers jeers, howls and execrations, some of them apt, some antagonistic and some obscene. She told the crowd that: "Humanity consists of two halves: men and women. One of these halves, man, as helpless by himself as one blade of a pair of scissors without the other, has no right to exclude the other half, woman, from a right to a voice in making the laws by which she is governed. Men who will not give women the rights of citizenship cannot complain if women become outlaws…Women are prepared to sacrifice their lives and property for humanity, men were prepared to sacrifice humanity in the interests of property."'

Leicester Pioneer Friday 13 June 1913.

Suffragettes in Bowling Green Street in May 1911, preparing for a demonstration with their new banner. On the left is Jane Wyatt, in the centre is Dorothy Pethwick and on the right is Miss Bowker.

Two men carry the Suffragettes' new banner in 1911. Mrs Hawkins is on the bottom right holding the rope.

Eleanor Glidewell addressing a very large crowd in June 1913. She was urging the crowd not to vote for the Liberal candidate. The poster is for a meeting to be addressed by George Lansbury. He had recently lost his parliamentary seat on the issue of votes for women and was in Leicester to support E.R. Hartley, the British Socialist Party candidate in the forthcoming parliamentary bye-election.

Bertha and Agnes Clarke selling the Suffragette *newspaper from a dog-cart in High Street, Leicester, c.1912. Bertha worked as a shoe machinist and her sister Agnes worked for a local laundry. Agnes had her first novel,* Glenroyst, *published in 1898. A year later her second novel,* Seven Girls, *appeared. This was about girls working in a laundry. Her third novel,* First Woman Minister, *was based on the Revd Gertrude von Petzold, who was appointed minister of Narborough Road Unitarian Church in 1904, thus becoming Britain's first woman minister.*

This undated photo of a tableau from the Equity Shoes works shows women as a worker, a bride, an academic or a teacher and as a symbol of liberty. Could this have been part of a Suffragette procession?

Miss Dorothy Pethick and Miss Bowker outside the WSPU premises at 14 Bowling Green Street, c.1914. Dorothy Pethick was the sister-in-law of Frederick Pethick-Lawrence who became a Leicester MP in 1923. The shop sold goods to help fund the cause.

Alice Hawkins (1863–1946) was one of Leicester's leading suffragettes. She went to prison five times for various acts committed as part of the WSPU's militant campaign for the vote. Mrs Hawkins was a mother of five children and worked as a machinist at Equity Shoes. She had been active in the ILP and in 1910 became president of the breakaway Independent National Union of Boot and Women Shoe Workers.

Alice Hawkins on her way to prison in July 1913, accompanied by Supt. Ward (in civilian clothes) and Supt. Carson. She had just been found guilty of pouring black ink into a post box on Friar Lane. Her sentence was 40s, or one month in prison. She chose prison.

Jane Wyatt was chair of the Leicester branch of the WSPU in 1913. She lived in the Belgrave area and taught at Harrison Road School.

This could be a May Day rally. On the left is the banner of the breakaway Women's Boot and Shoe Union. On the left of the ILP banner is the NUBSO banner with the shoemakers' patron St Crispin depicted in the middle portion.

Labour Sunday Celebrated.

The head of the May Day demonstration of 1914 passing through Humberstone Gate, led by (left to right) Messrs G. Black, G. Parbury, A.H. Harrison and George White.

The text of the resolution moved at the rally.

A view of the evening meeting with a platform consisting of four lorries fixed in front of the 'Golden Duke' statue.

Leicester Trades Council.

11, Briton Street.

Dear Sir,

The following resolution was passed at the last Council Meeting. If your Society approve of the same will you please send it on to the Town Clerk, Mr. H. A. Pritchard, Secretary of the Fixed Holidays Committee.

RESOLUTION.

"That this Society re-affirms its belief that the World's Recognised Labour Day (May 1st), should be established as a public holiday, and further instructs its representatives on the 'Fixed Holidays Committee' to move, that in any re-arrangement of holidays, this particular day should first be recognised as a general holiday."

Yours truly,

T. ROWLAND HILL, President.

J. H. BAUM, Secretary.

Above: Ramsay MacDonald addressing the 1916 Trades Council May Day Demonstration. Alderman Alf Hill can be seen behind him. Hill, who was opposed to the war, became MP for West Leicester in 1922.

Above: Ramsay MacDonald addressing the 1916 Trades Council May Day demonstration.

May 7/1916.

May Day Demonstration.

RESOLUTION.

"That this Mass Meeting of Leicester Trade Unionists looks with alarm upon the steady increase in the cost of the necessaries of life, which threatens to seriously lower the standards of the working classes; it feels that the conscription of wealth should precede any further conscription of the bodies of the people; it calls upon the Government to permanently nationalise the railways, control shipping, and take over such national industries as coal, clothing and food supply; it furthermore asks the wage-earners to rally round the Labour Movement, both, industrial and political, in order to protect themselves against exploitation and to prevent the conditions which will follow the War adding to their poverty."

To be Moved by ALDERMAN BANTON.

Seconded by COUNCILLOR A. HILL.

Supported by Mr. J. RAMSAY MACDONALD, M.P.

The text of the resolution, critical of conscription, being moved by the platform in the photos above and opposite. Conscription had been introduced in the spring of 1916.

MacDonald's Stand Against the War

MacDonald opposed Britain's entry into World War One and instead called for peace through negotiations. However, the majority of the Parliamentary Labour Party and the TUC supported the war effort. MacDonald's stance cost him dearly in the pro-war hysteria of the time. He became a pariah figure, ostracised, reviled and regarded by some as little less than a traitor. In the press he was accused of being a Bolshevik, a pacifist and of receiving German money.

In 1915 Labour joined the wartime coalition government led by Lloyd-George and played an active role in support of the war effort. The ILP not only opposed the war, but also opposed conscription. With the exceptions of Jabez Chaplin and T.F. Richards, this approach was supported by the bulk of the membership of the local branch. However, as the war progressed the atmosphere of jingoism prevailed and during the 1918 election hostile crowds frequently forced Ramsay MacDonald to abandon meetings. He was overwhelmingly defeated by I.F. Green, the candidate of the British Workers League that was little more than an anti-Labour front.

The war had ended the alliance between the Liberals and Labour, and an anti-Labour coalition between the Liberals and Conservatives was to be a continuing feature in local elections in Leicester.

The Town Hall, 1915. That year, the unwillingness of Leicester men to volunteer for the forces had become a public scandal. While in Nottingham and Newcastle 18 per cent of the men had volunteered, in Leicester the figure was only 2.6 per cent. The Town Council deplored the 'scanty response of Leicester men to recruiting appeals'.

Women working as cleaners on the Great Central Railway.

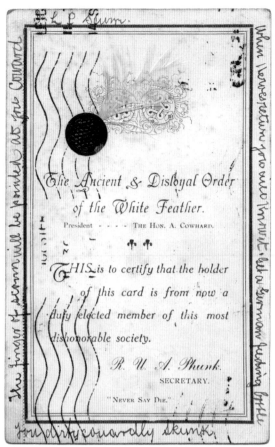

A card with no stamp and attached white feather was sent to the workplace of T.R. Hill, the secretary of the ILP.

Conscientious Objectors

By 1917 approximately 160 single and married members of the Leicester No-Conscription Fellowship had come under the Military Service Acts and had taken a stand as conscientious objectors. The Leicester branch of the fellowship was about 260 strong.

By August 1917 87 Leicester men had been arrested for evading conscription. These arrests had begun in early 1916 and continued through the rest of the war. Some of those arrested accepted non-combatant roles such as stretcher-bearers. Five could not endure solitary confinement at the barracks and also accepted non-combatant status after a few days. The rest were sent to Glen Parva, where they went through a 'very rough time' doing 'Field Punishment No.2'. These men were then drafted to various prisons and camps. Some refused to accept any compromise and continued in prison, with some on their second and third sentences.

In 1917 the organising secretary of the Leicester No-Conscription Fellowship, Horace Twilley, was serving 18 months hard labour in Welford Road prison with 16 other objectors. In the evening, their supporters would go to the prison wall and sing to them.

The ILP organiser, W.W. Borrett, also represented hundreds of men previously exempted for military service on medical grounds, who were called for re-examination.

A group of men who, in 1916, refused to be conscripted into the army on the grounds of conscience and chose to appear before the Leicester Tribunals.

Above: Queuing for bread in 1917. The ration had been reduced to 4lb of bread per week. As supplies were hit by submarine warfare, food prices rocketed and the local ILP campaigned against food profiteers and for a fairer system of rationing. Below: Queuing for margarine. For the first time in Britain, Leicester's Food Control Committee introduced the rationing of margarine and butter in 1917.

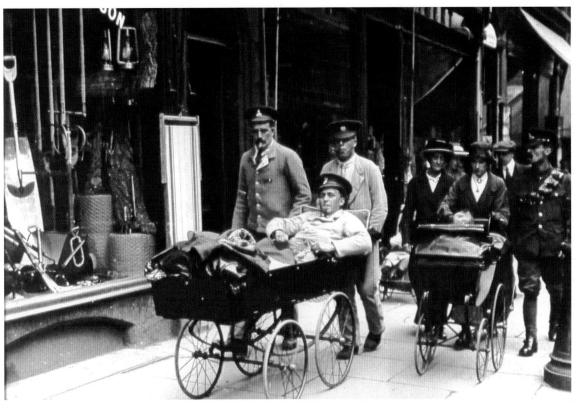

Above: A wounded soldier, reduced to helplessness, is pushed down Granby Street in a pram in 1918. He was one of 50,000 wounded who passed through the Base Hospital (the old County Lunatic Asylum, now the University of Leicester). By the end of the war, nearly three million British troops were listed as dead, wounded or missing.

Below: A May 1917 advert. MacDonald hoped that the first Russian revolution would usher in an era of democracy and that the Russian provisional government would create an impetus for peace negotiations. Instead it continued the war, providing the basis for the October Revolution.

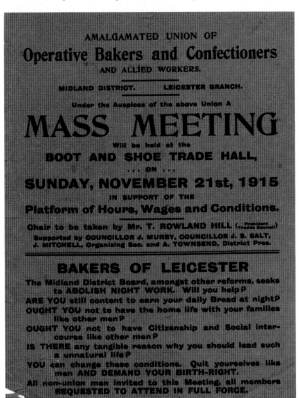

AMALGAMATED UNION OF

Operative Bakers and Confectioners

AND ALLIED WORKERS.

MIDLAND DISTRICT.   LEICESTER BRANCH.

Under the Auspices of the above Union A

MASS MEETING

Will be held at the

BOOT AND SHOE TRADE HALL,

... ON ...

SUNDAY, NOVEMBER 21st, 1915

IN SUPPORT OF THE

Platform of Hours, Wages and Conditions.

Chair to be taken by Mr. T. ROWLAND HILL (President).

Supported by COUNCILLOR J. MURBY, COUNCILLOR J. S. SALT, J. MITCHELL, Organising Sec. and A. TOWNSEND, District Pres.

BAKERS OF LEICESTER

The Midland District Board, amongst other reforms, seeks to ABOLISH NIGHT WORK. Will you help?

ARE YOU still content to earn your daily Bread at night?

OUGHT YOU not to have the home life with your families like other men?

OUGHT YOU not to have Citizenship and Social intercourse like other men?

IS THERE any tangible reason why you should lead such a unnatural life?

YOU can change these conditions. Quit yourselves like men AND DEMAND YOUR BIRTH-RIGHT.

All non-union men invited to this Meeting, all members REQUESTED TO ATTEND IN FULL FORCE.

P. SS THIS BILL ON TO A NON-UNION BAKER.

MAY-DAY

DEMONSTRATION

AND CELEBRATION OF THE

Russian Revolution

SUNDAY, MAY 6TH,

MARKET PLACE, 11 A.M.

Organised by the Trades Council.

SPEAKERS :—

J. R. MACDONALD, M.P.

ROBERT WILLIAMS,

Sec. Transport Workers' Federation.

THE PROCESSION

will assemble in Humberstone Gate at 9.45 and parade the principal streets.

YOU SHOULD JOIN IN.

John Riley (1855–1937) was a hosiery worker and member of the Hosiery Union Executive. As president of the Trades Council in 1918 he presided over the May Day meeting, which was effectively broken up by anti-MacDonald 'patriots.' He recounted that he had never forgotten the spectacle of the faces of men and women 'so distorted almost out of recognition by hatred and passion as on that day'.

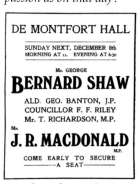

An advert for an election meeting in 1918.

Benjamin Russell's factory on Eastern Boulevard in November 1918.

The War Ends: Soldiers' Strikes of 1919

Private John Thomas Pantling (c.1887–1919) was a Socialist and member of the local Temperance movement in Belgrave. At the end of World War One he was co-founder of the Calais Soldiers and Sailors' Association. As their spokesman, he negotiated a reduction in the working week from 6½ to 6 days and better food and accommodation with the Army authorities. He also distributed the banned *Daily Herald* to troops in the area.

In January 1919 he was arrested for delivering a 'seditious' speech demanding demobilisation and was incarcerated in the Calais 'Bastille', where he faced court martial. When the news of Pantling's plight reached the Ordnance Depots, 4,000 troops marched behind brass bands towards the headquarters, which they quickly surrounded. A deputation successfully demanded his release and he was returned to his camp.

He was court martialled, but with some 20,000 men on strike in his support, he was acquitted. Just over a week later, he died from influenza and his comrades believed that his ill treatment while in prison was the main cause of his death.

Left: Private John Pantling.

Jabez Chaplin, a founder of the ILP and hosiery workers' leader, became mayor in 1919. Like Labour's parliamentary leaders, Chaplin was a strong supporter of the war effort. However, this led him to campaign against Ramsay MacDonald in support of the coalition candidate during the 'khaki' election of December 1918. This resulted in his expulsion from the Labour Party. Although the Labour nominee for mayor in 1919 was Amos Sherriff, the Council deemed that he was 'too unpatriotic' and elected Chaplin instead.

The advert reads:

DE MONTFORT HALL

SUNDAY NEXT, DECEMBER 8th
MORNING AT 11.   EVENING AT 6-30

Mr. GEORGE

BERNARD SHAW

ALD. GEO. BANTON, J.P.
COUNCILLOR F. F. RILEY
Mr. T. RICHARDSON, M.P.

Mr.

J. R. MACDONALD M.P.

COME EARLY TO SECURE
—A SEAT—

Leicester Trades Council

75 Branches.   43,000 Affiliated Members.

An Appeal to the Workers of Leicester.

THE Government, backed by all the Capitalist Forces of the country, are out to crush Trade Unionism. They have declared war on the railway workers. **What is the issue?**

THE ISSUE.

The Government proposals would have meant that certain grades of railway workers would have suffered a reduction of 14/- per week, making the minimum rate 40/-. **This, the railwaymen will not have.**

LLOYD GEORGE.

Mr. Lloyd-George says that the strike is the result of an "anarchist conspiracy." **It is a lie. It is used to deceive the people.**

THE PRESS.

The Press is being used by the Government. Lies are being poured out every day. They are the tools of the Capitalists of the country. They want to turn you against your fellow-workers.

Do not be deceived. The Railway Worker's fight is your fight. See that the truth is told. The railwaymen are solid throughout the land. See that your support is solid. The defeat of the railwaymen would be a death-blow to Trade Unionism.

Signed on behalf of the Leicester Trades Council :—

COUNCILLOR T. ADNITT (President).
FRANK ACTON (Vice-President).
W. H. LOWE, J.P. (Treasurer).
JAMES H. BAUM (Secretary).
A. MONK (Tramway Workers).
A. A. WEST (M.E.A.).
S. TAYLOR (Workers' Union).
E. BURNS (National Union of Railwaymen).
T. R. HILL (National Union of Clerks).
COUNCILLOR A. HILL (Boot and Shoe Operatives).
COUNCILLOR G. A. KENNEY (Trimmers).
COUNCILLOR N. C. PERKINS (Workers' Union).
JOHN RILEY (Hosiery Union).

The Blackfriars Press, Ltd. (46-hour week), 17 Albion Street, Leicester.

Rly Strike 1919   *1919*

Gathering fuel during the miners' strike of April 1921. The mine-owners had announced sweeping wage-cuts and posted lock-out notices at many pits. On 'Black Friday,' 15 April 1921, the leaders of the transport and rail unions refused to strike in support of their allies, the miners.

Left: An appeal for support from the Trades Council for the railwaymen during the national railway strike of September 1919. The rail unions claimed that the Government was applying a wartime pay agreement in such a way as to bring about wage cuts. The strike was to prove one of the most successful actions ever taken by the rail unions.

An election address for the 1920 council elections.

What LABOUR Stands For

HOUSES AND RENTS

The Labour Party desires to establish a housing minimum for the average family of no more than twelve houses to the acre (approximately 400 square yards for each house.) **The houses to be well planned, roomy, light and cheerful,** and consisting of not less than three bedrooms, bathroom, parlour, living room, scullery-kitchen, and **a good garden attached to each house.**

The houses would be designed and fitted to make the work of the housewife easier than it is in the ordinary house of to-day.

These houses are not too good for the worker. **The Rents must not be higher than for similar houses built before the war.**

To meet the need of old people the Labour Party desires special provisions to be made. The Labour Party will press for the speeding up of the Housing Schemes and Building by direct labour. **The Labour Party will also demand that property owners shall be compelled to decorate and repair houses when necessary.**

HEALTH

Health is wealth. The Labour Party is desirous of building an A1 Nation, and this can only be obtained through the following important measures :—

Safeguarding the child's future by insisting on healthy conditions, and the best Medical Service for expectant mothers.

A guaranteed supply, from birth onwards, of the necessaries of life, so as to ensure the full development of a sound and healthy body.

Maternity Homes, Child Welfare Centres, Day Nurseries, and a State Medical Service, are an absolute necessity under the present conditions.

Labour intends, however, to secure an "Ideal Home" for every Mother and Child.

The low standard of housing and factory conditions is largely responsible for Infantile Mortality and the alarming spread of consumption, which kills our fellow-citizens at the appalling rate of one per day.

Labour's Policy alone will secure a healthy, happy community.

EDUCATION

Knowledge is power. Ignorance is a curse. Education is a mighty lever for betterment, and this for centuries has been the monopoly of a privileged few. The Labour Party is striving to make Education—Education that enables the individual to realise the fullest and richest life—the birthright of all.

It would **abolish all fees,** and make the highway from the Elementary School to the University **absolutely free.**

Equal educational opportunity for all would be secured by making the ability to profit therefrom the sole test for entrance into the higher spheres of education.

Smaller Classes, Open-Air Schools, Maintenance Scholarships, Better Paid Teachers, and a more humane and liberal curriculum are all vital points in the Labour Party's present educational programme.

Labour's educational ideal is a healthy mind and a healthy body.

MUNICIPAL ENTERPRISE

The Labour Party believes that in the interest of the consumer the necessaries of life should be provided by the people at cost price.

It urges that the supply of Coal, Milk, and Bread should be undertaken on the co-operative principle by the City Council. **This would tend to lower prices and eliminate profiteering.**

The Labour Party also demands that public services, such as Gas, Electricity, Trams, be run for use and not for profit. To use profits for relief of rates is to rob the poor to relieve the rich.

The Labour Party is strongly in favour of cheap Allotments in permanent open spaces.

MUNICIPAL FINANCE

The Labour Party advocates the **Abolition of Rates** and the raising of local revenue by means of the Taxation of Land Values and an Income Tax on a graduated scale. No income under £250 to be taxed.

WORKERS—YOUR DUTY IS CLEAR—VOTE LABOUR

One of the leaders of the unemployed, Dennis Jennett, being arrested after the police broke up a demonstration in Rupert Street. He was sentenced to a month in prison.

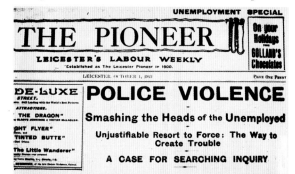

Leicester's Black Friday

On Friday 30 September 1921 a demonstration by the unemployed was broken up by the police outside the Poor Law Offices. The subsequent protest demonstrations led to a siege of the police station and left a trail of broken windows.

'I saw police chasing men along Horsefair Street after leaving Rupert Street and strike at them with their batons as they were running. I stood horror struck. I saw Dennis Jennett on the corner of Hotel Street and Horsefair Street; he was on his own gesticulating wildly, dishevelled and hatless. He was looking in the direction of Rupert Street and was shouting out: "Come along, boys; we will now show the dirty dogs what to do; come along with me to the (Corn) Exchange."

'This man could have easily been arrested; a mounted policeman jostled him along with his horse. The man then turned and proceeded to walk away towards the Market Place past Morgan Squires. As he was walking away a policeman walked up behind him and struck him with his baton. He lifted his baton for a second blow, but it was not necessary; the man was down and out.'

Charles Russell (*Leicester Pioneer*).

A deputation of 1,000 unemployed led by Charles Keene, senior, (X) meets the mayor on 26 September 1921. He had told the Guardians earlier: 'There is an enormous amount of unemployment and destitution. The position is getting worse because many of the men and women are ceasing to draw their benefit from the State and they feel something must be done to alleviate the sufferings of their families…If you gentlemen had undergone the experience of having nothing to eat, you might have more sympathy in a practical form with the starving men outside.'

The Poor Law in the 1920s

The workhouse (renamed the Swain Street Institution) continued as an instrument of the Poor Law throughout the 1920s. Not only were the Tory/Liberal majority of Leicester's elected Poor Law Guardians themselves reluctant to provide assistance to those in need except through relief in kind (usually bread), they were also prevented from doing so by Government rules.

Following the 1921 demonstrations, the work schemes pioneered by Amos Sherriff and the Labour Guardians did at least reward the unemployed with wages half in kind and half in money.

Left: The stone breaking cell at the workhouse in 1921. Paupers were locked in this cell and had to feed the broken rocks through a hole on to the yard below.

Below: Amos Sherriff, in his mayoral year, hands out Christmas dinners at the workhouse in 1922.

Catherine Irwin (left) was a Labour Guardian and Amos Martin (right) was leader of the Labour Guardians.

Staff of the Leicester Co-operative Society Tailoring Department in 1920.

The 1920 May Day procession in High Street.

The Corn Mill, Ash Street, c.1915.

A Co-op float in the 1920 May Day procession.

A Butchery Department delivery van, c.1915.

The Central Butchery Store, High Street and Cart's Lane, 1923.

S.G. Woolley was a founder of Equity shoes and a board member of the Leicester Co-operative Society.

An unidentified Co-op store.

Edwin Baum was a founder member of the ILP and a board member of the Leicester Co-op during the 1920s.

The Co-op bakery in 1923.

Advertisement, 1922.

March 1922: George Banton MP

'One thing now becoming quite evident was that war passions were gradually subsiding…the industrial depression with the unemployment and misery that it entailed amongst the masses of the people was changing the public attitude to the hard-faced industrialists who swarmed into Parliament in 1918, as a bye-election in the East Division of Leicester in March 1922 abundantly demonstrated. Alderman George Banton was again the Labour candidate and he won the seat with a majority of 1,500 over his combined Liberal and Tory opponents.'

William Howard (Labour organiser)

Alderman George Banton MP with William Howard, the Labour organiser, outside the Labour Party offices in Rutland Street sometime in the 1920s.

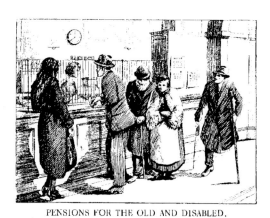

Illustrations from George Banton's 1922 election address.

George Banton's 1922 election address.

West Leicester General Election Success, November 1922: Alf Hill MP

In the November 1922 general election George Banton was defeated in East Leicester (he later retook the seat). However, in West Leicester Alf Hill, a local councillor, Methodist preacher and clicker in the boot and shoe trade, was elected. Alf Hill had been prominent in NUBSO since the 1890s and had taken a firm stand against the war. According to the *Leicester Pioneer:*

'On the first Sunday in August 1914, he felt compelled to leave his religious work and take part in a political demonstration on a Sunday...No orator thrilled the crowd as Alfred Hill did. He spoke with a fervour and passion that told of the fierce earnestness of his soul, against the black hellish horror through which the nations of the world have since passed. He spoke for peace, as a man inspired, and no jingo raised his voice for war on that memorable day.

In the war that followed, he never wavered in his stand for peace and although it meant a certain amount of unpopularity and brought on his shoulders a certain amount of abuse, he came through as a man who could stand for great religious and political principles.'

A local election leaflet for Maria Leafe, 1925.

Labour's first woman councillor Emily Fortey (1866–1946) was elected in 1923. She was a devout Catholic and always wore a semi-religious outfit. Although women had been able to stand for election to the council from 1907, it was not until 1922 that Mrs Ellan Swanston was elected as an independant.

Councillor Alf Hill, c.1912.

Municipal Election, 1925.   Aylestone Ward.

What LABOUR has done for Aylestone!

More has been done for Aylestone Ward during the last 2 years than for 20 years previous.

Aylestone now has a **splendid water supply**, a special tank having been built to hold over a million gallons.

Aylestone now has its own **Baby Clinic**, where mothers can take their little ones for free treatment.

Old Aylestone has its own **Polling Station**, thanks to the efforts of a Labour Councillor.

Aylestone's Library has been overhauled, painted and new electric lights installed.

The mortuary is to be removed.

New Bridge for Old Aylestone, two new bridges in Knighton Lane and the Railway Bridge is to have attention. The new estate means prosperity for Aylestone shop-keepers.

Saffron Lane Brook was to have had attention, but was thrown out by our opponents.

Aylestone Streets are better lighted, and its roads and pavements have been improved.

Lansdowne Road and Granby Road Schools have never had such attention, class rooms, lavatories, ground extensions, school equipment and motor signs.

Landlords have been compelled to repair their property and have nuisances of lavatories, drains and roofs put right.

Factories sending out **Black Smoke** in Aylestone have been warned or prosecuted.

Old age pensioners' interests have been watched.

Milk supplied to Tubercular men, women and children. Necessitous cases have had milk for their babies.

We have fought for and **obtained better pensions** for long service workmen. We have opposed the reduction of wages to workers. We have consistently opposed **increases of salaries** to big officials.

All these things and more have your Labour Councillors done for Aylestone Ward. Send **Mrs. Leafe** to help **Councillor Keene** carry on.

The Conservatives have one Councillor. What has he done?

VOTE LABOUR and get SERVICE.

Printed & Published by Newman Wolsey & Co., Printers, &c., 27-29 Millstone Lane, Leicester.

A Co-operative Village Industry

Wigston Hosiers was formed in 1897 and started trading in 1899, having bought six Griswold machines on the advice of George Newell of the Leicester Hosiery Society. The business flourished and in 1905 the Co-operative bought a plot of land in Paddock Street and built a factory. By 1910 this factory was too small and a new factory was built in 1913. In those days the factory looked out over gardens and orchards stretching down to the houses in the old part of the village.

In 1914 the factory specialised in men's half hose, shirts, pants and combinations, children's socks and ladies' cashmere hose. All the workers at the factory were in the union, working 49 hours per week and being paid the Leicester rate, even though Wigston was considered to be a country district. The society continued to prosper throughout the inter-war years and celebrated its 50th anniversary in 1949.

The first factory of the Wigston Hosiers Ltd in 1899. This factory was in Bull's Head Street.

The second Wigston Hosiers factory in Paddock Street in 1905.

A show card from the 1920s.

The third Wigston Hosiers factory in Paddock Street in 1921.

The hosiery and underwear finishing room at Wigston Hosiers Ltd, c.1920.

Underwear machinery at Wigston Hosiers Ltd, c.1920.

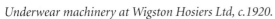

Hosiery winding machinery at Wigston Hosiers Ltd, c.1920.

Automatic machinery at Wigston Hosiers Ltd, c.1920.

J.J.Worley (1876–1944) was regarded as an ambassador for co-operative production throughout Europe. He worked for the Leicester-based Co-operative Productive Federation, whose job it was to foster co-operatively run factories.

He was a fluent public speaker and, addressing the gathering at the co-operators Day celebrations at De Montfort Hall in 1930, he told the audience that the 'Leicestershire miner would have more in common with the German miner than he would with his fellow countryman the Duke of Northumberland. The Duke and the miners lived in different worlds.' During the 1930s he was active in the anti-fascist cause.

Top to bottom:
The Glenfield Progress Co-operative Boot Society works, c.1927. The previous year the factory had supplied striking miners families with boots and shoes at cost price.

The new Excelsior Co-operative Boot and Shoe factory in Sileby, c.1925.

The composing department at the Leicester Co-operative Printers, Churchgate, in 1923.

The machine department at the Leicester Co-operative Printers.

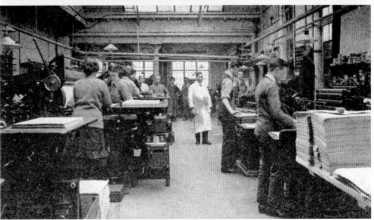

Specialist Motor Body and Carriage Builders

This unusual co-operative enterprise was founded in 1903. It was a bold venture and the only society of its kind in the co-operative market. It began trading from premises on Thornton Lane and as the business expanded it moved to Highcross Street and later East Bond Street.

In 1913 the Carriage Builders moved to purpose-built premises on Marlow Road comprising offices, workshop and wood mill, with a blacksmiths shop at the rear. For many years the society was governed on democratic lines with the profits being divided between capital, custom and worker.

By the 1930s it had an established reputation for building bakers' vans (on pneumatic tyres), travelling butchers' and grocers' shops, drapery and hardware vans, and all kinds of vehicles for Co-op dairies. These could be built on to any make of chassis.

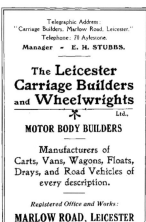

An advert from 1915.

Above: A motor van built in 1923.
Below: A charabanc, probably built in the late 1920s. The business is now part of the Midlands Co-op and is still on Marlow Road, where it makes mobile libraries, accessible community transport and play vehicles.

'The splendid specimens of babyhood pointed to the obvious advantages that all babies had who were fed on such pure food as the Leicester Co-operative Society's Pasteurised Milk,' claimed the Leicester Co-operative Magazine. These proud mothers were at the Baby Show at the Co-operators' Day Fête at De Montfort Hall in 1923. The increasing use of dried and pasteurised milk was responsible for a drop in infant mortality.

Below: The Co-op store in High Street decked out in gala attire for International Co-operator's day in July 1924.

Frederick Pethick-Lawrence MP at the annual Labour gala at De Montfort Hall Gardens in July 1928.

Fredrick Pethick-Lawrence had a sensational victory when he beat Winston Churchill in West Leicester in 1923. Before World War One, Pethick-Lawrence had been imprisoned with his wife for conspiracy as a result of their role in the campaign for women's suffrage. He was defeated in the 1931 election.

Gooding Avenue, South Braunstone Estate, built in the late 1920s.

Although council-house building on the Coleman Road estate had been started at the end of World War One, it was not until 1924 that any large schemes got underway. By this time there was a chronic shortage of housing in the city. Inspired by the garden city ideal, the new estates at Saffron Lane and South Braunstone were built from 1924 onwards. However, high rents meant that this improved standard of housing was still out of the reach of many of the very poor families, who stayed in the city's slums. Nevertheless, many better-off working families started to move from the city centre out to the new estates.

Housing and Town Planning Committee, c.1928.

Councillor Herbert Hallam (1877–1933) was strongly influenced by the Garden City movement. In 1914 he successfully proposed that the council should start a housing scheme, but it was delayed by the war. In 1924 he became Chairman of the Housing Committee and was responsible for the planning and building of the Saffron Lane and South Braunstone estates. He opposed Government pressure to build small council houses and instead advocated the 'parlour' house, with two downstairs living rooms.

Above: The Park Estate, Saffron Lane, being built in 1925. This large estate was made possible by the 1924 Housing Act passed by the first Labour government. Below: The Park Estate (Saffron Lane) was the city's first large-scale council estate. However, the desperate need for homes and the shortage of labour and materials meant that non-traditional concrete houses were seen as the solution. These 'Boot' homes lasted until the 1990s when they had to be demolished for structural reasons.

Above: Newly-completed houses on the Braunstone Estate in March 1932. At this time the roads were still unmade and they remained so for some time, despite protests from the tenants.

Below: These council houses on the South Braunstone Park Estate were built under the terms of the 1924 Wheatley Housing Act. They were designed by the council's housing architect, J.S. Fyfe, and built c.1929–30. As well as upstairs bathrooms and toilets, they also had a separate bicycle store. They featured real half timbering, indoor toilets and a parlour room. They are now the subject of a preservation order.

The Co-operative Garage in Ash Street in 1923. The smaller vans were British-built Fords and the larger vehicles were Leylands. The Co-operative Leicester Carriage Builders adapted vehicles to provide travelling shops for the Butchery Department.

A newly-built Co-op store on the Fair Way on the Park Estate, Saffron Lane. It was built by the Co-op's own building department to the designs of the CWS architects. The shop boasted a butchery and grocery department with a bacon-slicing machine of the 'most modern type'. Opening the shop in November 1926 Amos Mann said: 'The shops that were to be opened stood for the Movement which intended to abolish that state of society in which men worked for private profit and to establish a system in which they strove to supply the needs of people so that everyone obtained a like advantage.' That year the Co-op opened branches at Birstall and on Holbrook Road, Knighton.

According to the Leicester Mail: 'Major Murray-Smith, son of Hon. Mrs Murray-Smith, is a volunteer guard on the L.M.S., and is doing his work exceptionally well. Here he is signalling out the London-Manchester train at Leicester this afternoon. His father was once chairman of the Midland railway.'

The strikebreakers were not very competent railwaymen. This derailment of petrol wagons at Loughborough station during the strike was from a train manned by 'volunteers'.

A pirate bus to Stoneygate plies for trade. The Tramways Committee, chaired by George Banton, had decided not to run any trams during the strike. This avoided any conflict between strikers and 'volunteers', but upset his Conservative colleagues.

Leicestershire miners collecting strike pay.

A.J. Cook, the miners' leader, in Coalville.

A miner's family meal with largely bread to eat.

Leicestershire miners tramp to the Leicester Labour Gala in June 1926. By this time many of their colleagues had returned to work.

George Parbury joined NUBSO in 1889 and took part in the great lock-out of 1895. He joined the ILP the same year. In 1905 he became a permanent official of NUBSO and was secretary of No.1 Branch from 1912. This branch had 10,000 members and was thought to be the largest trade union branch in the world. He was elected to the town council in 1921 for Abbey ward and served into the 1940s, becoming Lord Mayor in 1939.

Thomas Adnitt (b.1868) went into the boot and shoe trade in 1896. He was later sacked as a result of trade union activity and was elected as a full-time union official in March 1919. He was also a member of the union's national executive. He was elected president of the Trades Council in 1919 and was a Labour town councillor for Belgrave and Latimer. Despite being crippled by an accident in early life, he was secretary of a swimming club.

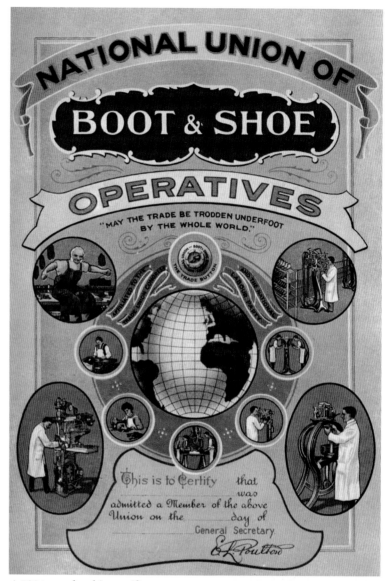

A 1924 membership certificate.

Right: This undated hand-tinted photograph is of Mrs Mary Bell-Richards, the leader of the women's branch of NUBSO. Her flamboyant outfit was well matched to the wardrobe of her husband, T.F. Richards, who was regarded as the Beau Brummell of the trade union movement. The strong bargaining position of women in Leicester and the pugnacity of Mrs Bell-Richards ensured that women's wages in the shoe trade rose from 56 per cent of the men's rate to 67 per cent in 1935. She also fiercely contested the notion that working women could not be good mothers.

James Baum (b.1878) was the son of a quarry worker. He was brought up in Mountsorrel by his grandfather, who had been a staunch Chartist. James Baum joined NUBSO No.2 Branch in 1896 and was elected secretary of the Trades Council in 1912. He held that position for 11 years. He eventually became the National Organiser of NUBSO. He joined the ILP in 1900 and after World War One he acted as agent in West Leicester for Alf Hill MP and later Frederick Pethick-Lawrence MP.

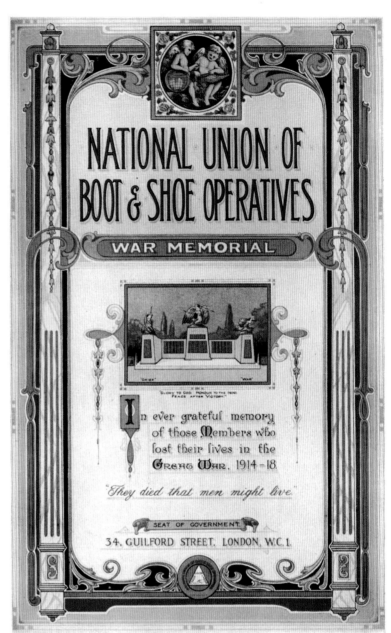

E.L. Poulton, the general secretary of NUBSO, 1908–30. On his election as general secretary of NUBSO he moved to Leicester from Northampton, where he had been mayor. In 1921 he became chairman of the TUC.

Dominic (Dan) McCarthy (c.1862–1937) was born in Ireland and joined NUBSO in 1892. He worked as a shoe laster at the CWS Wheatsheaf works. In 1895 he was elected to the Trades Council and was an ILP member of the Board of Guardians for 18 years. He was member of the board of the Leicester Co-operative Society in 1919 when he was elected as a national organiser of NUBSO. He helped initiate the daily delivery of milk to Co-op customers.

In 1900 W.E. Wilford (b.1879) was a businessman and a rising hope of the Liberal Party. However, his experience of organising meals for poor children during 1904–06 led him to think about the causes of poverty and he defected to Labour, founding the South Leicester Labour Church. He was elected to the council in 1912 and was Lord Mayor in 1931.

T. Rowland Hill (1885–1968) was president of the Trades Council in 1914 and its secretary from 1925–32. He was secretary of the ILP in 1917 and was also a director of the Co-operative Society. He was elected to the city council in 1930 and was chairman of the Finance Committee from 1934 until 1955. He became Lord Mayor in 1951.

Charles Edward Keene (senior) (1868–1953) was born on a sailing ship en route to India. He came to Leicester from Bradford with 6s in his pocket in 1899 and successfully established several different businesses in the city, which included the Mutual Clothing and Supply Company. He was a lifelong supporter of the temperance movement and acted as spokesman for the unemployed in 1921. He was elected to the city council for Aylestone in 1924.

Sam Cooper came to Leicester in 1914 and worked as a ticket collector on the railways. He was an active member of the NUR and was elected to the Board of Guardians in 1925. In 1930 he was elected from Charnwood ward to the city council, becoming an alderman in 1952 and Lord Mayor in 1955.

Harry Hand (b.1865) was the eldest child of a large family and attended Charnwood Street Board School. He was at work as a part-timer at the age of eight and left school at 11. He was a carpenter by trade, joining the Carpenters and Joiners Union in 1886 and was a councillor for Abbey ward from 1909–45.

Ernest Grimsley (b.1873) was one of nine children. He was a Methodist lay preacher and was a strong advocate of temperance. He joined the Typo-graphical Association (print union) in 1894 and was elected to the town council for Labour in 1919.

Charles Keene (junior) in 1927. His career on the council continued until the 1960s.

John Minto was a councillor from 1922 until the 1950s. He was parliamentary candidate for Bosworth during the 1920s, only losing by a couple of hundred votes. He became leader of the council in the early 1950s.

Cllr Walter Oram was a local businessman.

Above and below: Cartoons from Conservative election broadsheets of 1928. In reality, local Labour politicians were a highly respectable mixture of trade union officials and local businessmen. During the 1920s and 1930s the issues of slum clearance and council house building became Labour's flagship policies. Although it was a hung council, Labour councillor frequently chaired the major committees.

NEW INDUSTRY SAYS "SAFETY FIRST."

THE LORD MAYOR : "Welcome to Leicester. Just the place for your factories."
MR. NEW INDUSTRY : "We like the look of Leicester, *but* how do we know we won't be attacked if we do settle here ?"

'Is this our Leicester?' asks a Tory election leaflet, as Socialism sneaks towards municipal office in 1928. Simon de Montfort, Cardinal Wolsey and Lady Jane Grey look distinctly put out.

The last council meeting in the old Council Chamber on 28 July 1931. The Labour group is on the left of the picture with Emily Fortey in the foreground sitting next to T.F. Richards and the aldermen are sat on either side of the Lord Mayor. There are just three women in the picture. After the opening of the new Council Chamber, this room was used as a court until 1992.

A tug of war at the Labour Gala in De Montfort Hall Gardens in 1928.

The Labour Party's annual fund-raising event was the Labour Gala, where political speeches would be mixed in with dance bands, tombola and a fancy dress competition. Left: Frederick and Emmeline Pethick-Lawrence at the 1928 Labour Gala. Below: Herbert Morrison MP with Labour agent Walter Lewis at the Labour Gala in 1929. The following year the official guest was the up and coming Labour politician Oswald Mosley.

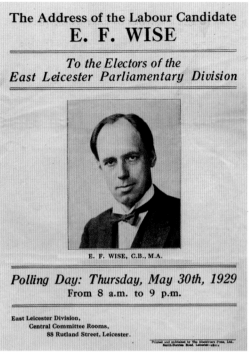

Election posters can be still seen plastered on the corner of Wilton Street and Belgrave Gate, October 1929. Note the 'Vote Labour' and 'No More War' posters. There is also a poster for the annual Co-op fête and one for the second talking picture: 'Syncopation'.

Former civil servant Frank Wise was elected MP for East Leicester in 1929, but lost his seat in the 1931 general election. In 1932 he helped found the left-wing Socialist League at the Labour Party Conference held in Leicester.

Two women winding yarn on to bobbins at the Harrison and Hayes factory in Asylum Street in 1928. During the years of the depression, Leicester's hosiery industry fared better than most. As pullovers and cardigans became popular with both sexes, so the demand for knitwear increased. New fashions in short skirts and silk and rayon stockings also helped local industry. 'Leicester Clothes the World' was the slogan adopted by the Leicester Chamber of Commerce.

The Co-op first set up a dairy in 1903. The New Model Dairy on Glenfield Road was opened in November 1929. With a new bottling plant, the Co-op was now able to deliver its milk in bottles.

Milk deliveries in Severn Street (previously Mecklenberg Street) in 1929.

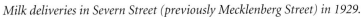

The opening of the new Belgrave Co-op shops on the Loughborough Road, May 1932.

Left: The opening of the Co-op shops at the Aylestone tram terminus, 1931.

Right: The newly-opened Co-op chemists on the Belgrave Road. It

had previously been a Co-op café and was converted by the Co-op building department using the 'most up-to-date methods of shop designing'.

The Welford Road Co-op, opened in March 1928.

Above: The Braunstone Co-op Store, Hallam Crescent East, opened in 1930. The four-faced clock on the roof was synchronised with the one in the manager's office.

The Co-op's new laundry on Gypsy Lane in 1929. Before the advent of washing machines, the Co-operative Laundry was a boon to working women. It was so popular that it could not always meet the demand for its services.

Right: An advertisement from 1939.

Below: Co-op members at their annual tea in De Montfort Hall in July 1928.

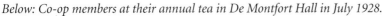

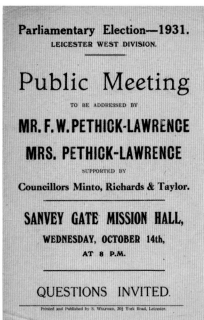

Election leaflet.

1931: Defeat and Betrayal

'The defection of MacDonald…was a bitter blow to the Labour Party supporters in Leicester, for in this city he had been idolised to a degree higher than his merits warranted by people within the Party and many thousands outside. It is not to be wondered at, therefore, that in the election of 1931 the Party suffered a very severe reverse; the East and West Divisions were lost by tremendous adverse majorities and our vote in the South was very much reduced. The election was exceptionally bitter particularly in the East and the South where vicious personal attacks were made on E.F. Wise and John Dugdale. Fear and panic engendered by an unscrupulous press and by renegade leaders, for the time being at least, made democracy safe for Toryism, but it must never be forgotten that in Leicester where adoration of MacDonald had nearly reached the level of a cult, 36,000 people stood firm for Socialism, and it is a matter for pride that not one prominent member of the Party in Leicester followed MacDonald into the Tory camp.'

William Howard (Labour Organiser).

The National Unemployed Workers' Movement protest at the cut in unemployment pay.

A cartoon from a 1931 Conservative leaflet. F. Pethick-Lawrence is shown as an old woman, referring to his involvement with the Suffragettes. 'Frank' is Leicester East MP E.F. Wise.

Children carrying banners in support of Labour during the 1931 election.

Above: In January 1932, the NUWM organised a funeral procession from the Market Place for one of its young members. The ILP Guild of Youth claimed that his death was due to starvation due to the Means Test, a claim that was vehemently denied by officials at the Public Assistance Office.

The Means Test

In 1931 the national Government cut unemployment benefit. It imposed a means test on claimants and withdrew benefit until savings were spent or furniture sold. Thousands of people now had to account for every single penny that came into their household and declare it to inspectors.

Relief for the unemployed was administered by local Public Assistance Committees composed of local councillors. In October Amos Sheriff, the vice-chairman of the committee, proposed that the Leicester committee should not work the Means Test. This was voted down by the Liberals and Tories and, according to Emily Fortey, 'we were defeated and the question arose as to what our attitude should be. We felt rightly or wrongly that by working in with others we should prevent a great deal of hardship, because local authorities can work this means test humanely within certain limits, or just the reverse. We knew exactly what would happen if we had left it entirely to the Tories and Liberals'.

However, the NUWM continued to press the council not to operate the Means Test. Claud Boat, spokesman for the unemployed, told the press: 'We are speaking for a thousand Leicester people who marched through the streets this afternoon and 5,000 who listened to us and who are definitely behind us. We claim people inside and outside our organisation are not getting a decent standard of livelihood where the Means Test is applied. We say it is a damnable thing.'

Left: Tom Richards of the NUWM addresses a crowd in the Market Place.

The 1931 Bedeaux Strike

In December 1931, the management at the Wolsey factory introduced the American Bedeaux productivity system at its Coalville factory. The Coalville 'girls' refused to work it and were promptly locked out by the company.

With union support, workers at the giant Abbey Park Road factory went on strike and for eight weeks the union supported almost the entire workforce of 2,000 women and 1,000 men.

There was considerable public support for the strike and hostility to the imported American wage system. Eventually the management gave way and on 10 February the strike ended when the firm agreed to alter the Bedeaux system. The union had won significant concessions, though it was not a conclusive victory.

Strikers leaving a meeting held at the Corn Exchange in January 1932. Union secretary Horace Moulden argued that the dispute had not been inspired by union officials, but had arisen from the workers' bitter experiences: 'they know what it means if they lose the fight and have to work under the system. The whole country is watching Leicester'.

Wolsey workers outside De Montfort Hall following the ending of the strike in February 1932. The Hosiery Union could claim that it had won significant concessions from the employers.

The Demise of the ILP

Disappointed with the record of the previous Labour government, the ILP disaffiliated from the Labour Party in 1932. However, its local councillors, including T.F. Richards, W.H. Smith and Emily Fortey, chose to stay in the Labour Party.

After an absence of 22 years, Labour veteran T.F. Richards was elected back on to the city council in 1929.

With its local membership split, the local organiser Will Owen was dispensed with and the party's premises were closed. When the ILP stood in the 1933 local elections in Castle ward it polled just 80 votes.

Although the red shirts of the ILP Guild of Youth became a familiar sight on anti-fascist demonstrations, the ILP had consigned itself to the political fringes.

May Day, 1933: a Co-op float.

Horace Moulden, the leader of the Hosiery Union, addressing workers at Ratby during the Wolsey dispute of 1931–32.

T.F. Richards addressing the May Day rally in 1932.

A contingent of Leicester's unemployed joined the hunger march that passed through the city in the autumn of 1932.

The 1934 Hunger March

Hunger marchers on Belgrave Road on 14 February 1934.

The 1934 Hunger March was one of several protest marches that passed through Leicester in the 1930s. A reception committee had booked Granby Halls for the marchers, but the Council's Public Assistance Committee refused to provide the men with blankets unless they entered the workhouse.

When the marchers arrived, women church members helped volunteer ambulance nurses and tend the marchers' sore feet. They were bathed and massaged so thoroughly that one man said that walking on the road again was like walking on carpet. They were given tea at the schoolroom of St Mark's Church where one room was turned into a first-aid post. Another room was used as a library, where 100 men wrote letters home on paper provided and a concert was given in a third room.

Wearing the daffodils given to them at St Mark's, the marchers held a parade in the town. Following a special meeting of the Council's Baths and Sanitary Committee, the marchers were given free use of the public baths, but the Public Assistance Committee's refusal to supply blankets meant that the marchers spent two nights at the Swain Street Institution.

Hunger marchers getting tea at St Mark's Church in February 1934.

The hunger marchers crossing Swain Street Bridge on the way from the workhouse, where they had just spent the night.

The Unemployed Movement

In comparison with other areas, Leicester's economy in the 1930s was relatively prosperous. There was unemployment in the town, but it did not reach catastrophic proportions. Nevertheless, when 140 men were wanted for snow clearing in February 1933, 1,000 men besieged the Corporation's Grape Street depot. Police had to be brought in to guard the depot's gates and to protect the men taken on.

Although the local unemployed movement remained small, it was very vociferous. The NUWM was viewed with some suspicion by the majority of the Trades Council because many of its activists were drawn from the Communist Party.

Early in 1932, an Unemployed Social Council was instigated by the local Free Church Council and shortly after the hunger marchers arrived in Leicester in 1932 it held a 'Cornflower Flag Day' to finance its activities. By the end of the year it had opened centres for the unemployed in Churchgate and in Overton Road. As well as providing social facilities, various classes were run and tools, seeds and allotments were supplied. Centres for the unemployed were also set up by the council.

A black coffin was on view at an unemployed demonstration on Good Friday, c.1935.

A meeting of the unemployed in the Market Place in May 1934. Local Communist Dave Shepherd is on the left of the picture.

Ellen Wilkinson MP arriving in Leicester in October 1936 with the Jarrow Marchers.

A march of the unemployed on 9 May 1934 led by the Leicester Unemployed Broad Council.

Slum Clearance in the 1930s

The 1930 Housing Act made it possible for a start to be made on clearing some of Leicester's slum housing. The first clearance area was Abbey Street and Mansfield Street, where there were back-to-back houses, shared outside toilets and houses with no internal sinks or water supply. Politically it was not a straightforward process as landlords resisted demolition. The local Tories were anxious not to offend their natural supporters and consequently opposed Labour's more radical approach.

Left: 8-10 St Peters Lane (between Highcross and North Bond Street). These small houses shared a common yard and had a huge factory girder in front of the bedroom windows. They were due for clearance in 1934, but landlords successfully appealed against their demolition in the County Court. Eventually, the council got its way and the tenants were rehoused in 1938 and the houses demolished later that year.

Below: This view shows Charter Street Court A at the back of 9–13 Caroline Street (off Archdeacon Lane leading to Gas Street), complete with fractured and perished brickwork. On the right was one of two back-to-back houses in the court. Two water taps and three WCs were shared by the nine households. The tenants were rehoused on Hand Avenue in 1937 and the court was demolished in February 1938.

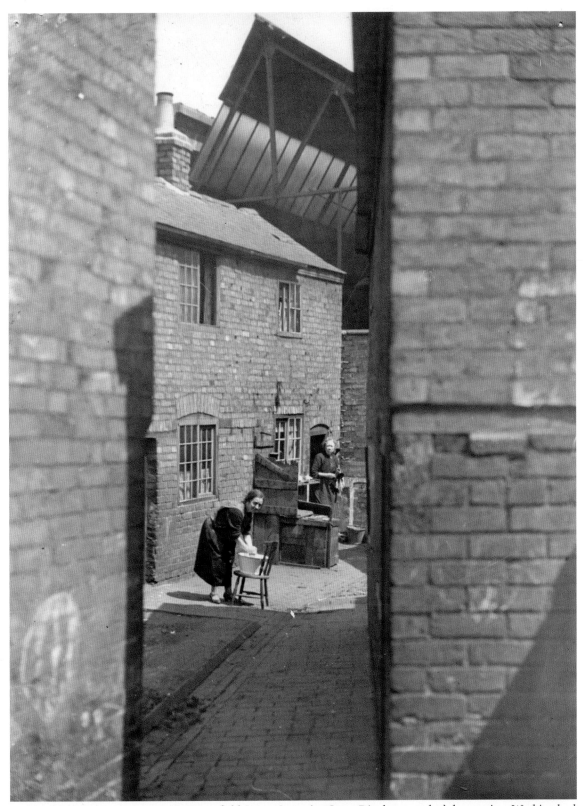

A view through the narrow entry to Mansfield Street Court (or Court D), close to today's bus station. Washing had to be done outside because it is likely that these cottages had no sink or internal water supply. The factory in the background was probably the bottling plant on the corner of Abbey and Mansfield Street. This area was Leicester's first slum clearance scheme and these slum dwellers were rehoused in new council houses on Martival/Overton Road during the summer of 1932. These slum cottages were demolished a few months later.

Slum dwellers in the Abbey Street area.

Sandacre Street, Bailey's Yard, c.1930. These houses had to share one tap and an outside gully. Common WCs are in the foreground on the right and further back there is a three-storey hosiery factory. These houses were back-to-back with houses facing onto Lower Sandacre Street. This courtyard was demolished in December 1932. The tenants were rehoused on Martival/Overton Road where they paid a rent of 10s 6d per week.

Life in the Slums

'You used to step straight in from the street to the living room. A wooden table stood in the middle, there was the old fire grate with hobs and ovens and a sink in the corner which did for everything. There was no kitchen, it wasn't even curtained off. There was a very cold brick stone floor which you had to scrub – you couldn't put lino down. This floor was covered by peg rugs which were made by me dad. He did the cooking and tucked us in at night. There was just one bedroom upstairs. Old wooden stairs with no carpet on led to the single bedroom…We used to have a big double bed one end and another one the other, I suppose that was my mum and dad's and there were three of us then – three in a bed. I can remember baby…must have slept with my mum and dad, because there was no way you could have got a cot in. In fact we never used to be able to get out of bed normal, like we do now – we had to clamber over the other beds. That's all it was: one up and one down – everything in the one room…'

Mrs Hall on life in West Short Street.

Looking up Gravel Street towards Churchgate from the location of today's bus station, c.1931. A man changes the wheel on the Leicester Co-operative Printing Society's lorry at the back of the printing works. You can just see the crack in the defective brickwork on the house on the corner of Short Street.

This photograph shows the back kitchen of 8 Queen Mary Street, sometime in the 1930s. In the low-ceilinged kitchen you can see the copper, fireplace and kitchen utensils. It was so small it had to be photographed from the next room. Although the picture was taken on a bright sunny day, little light was able to penetrate the gloom of this house.

Council houses on the Tailby Estate, built in the early 1930s for displaced slum dwellers from the centre of town.

Penny Bank Galas

In 1873 the Leicester Co-operative Society established a Children's Penny Bank, which was intended as a way of instilling the notion of thrift into the young. The bank was also a means by which the Society accumulated capital and it proved to be a source of strength in times of difficulty.

The 1934 Penny Bank Gala, at which 4,000 young Co-operators were entertained on the Aylestone Agricultural Ground by Punch and Judy shows, clowns and bands. Over 20,000 cakes and 10,000 bars of chocolate were eaten during the free tea.

The procession from Freeschool Lane to the 1930 Penny Bank Gala at Aylestone Road Agricultural Ground.

The Humberstone Road Co-op grocery store, probably in 1931.

This 1931 window display at the Humberstone Road Co-op grocery store was for 'Lutona', which was the Co-op's own brand of cocoa, made at its factory in Luton.

Interior of the Central Grocery Department, High Street, Leicester, 1933.

The interior of the Boot and Shoe Department, High Street, Leicester, 1933.

Below left: The High Street hairdressers, 1925.
Below right: First-floor dining room and café, High Street central store, 1933.

Fascism in Leicester

In March 1933, the *Leicester Mercury* urged its readers to 'give Mr Hitler a chance'. At that time, such sympathetic press coverage for Nazi Germany was not unusual. In 1935 the persecution of Jews and trade unionists led the Trades Council to call for a boycott of German goods, but such opposition was confined to the left.

From 1934–39 there was an active local branch of the British Union of Fascists. However, its attempts to hold meetings in the Market Place met with hostile crowds and eventually the police banished the BUF to the Haymarket in order to keep the peace. Mosley and his followers also held carefully stewarded meetings in various public halls. Often, hostile questioners were set upon by his blackshirts. With Labour's abandonment of street politics, it was left to the Co-op Party, the local Jewish community, the ILP and Communist Party to organise the opposition.

A heckler escorted away by police after having been ejected by blackshirts from Mosley's 1936 rally at Granby Halls.

Left: An advertisement for a rally in 1935.

YOU ARE INVITED TO HEAR

SIR OSWALD MOSLEY

EXPLAIN

FASCIST POLICY

At the GRANBY HALLS, LEICESTER,

On SUNDAY, APRIL 14th,

at 8 p.m. (doors open 7.15).

ADMISSION FREE. Reserved seats at 6d. to 2s. 6d., obtainable from:—
W. H. RUSSELL & SONS, 99, Granby Street, Leicester, or
B.U.F., Florence Building, St. Nicholas Street, or
90, Humberstone Road, Leicester.

Below: Roland Walton addresses a meeting of anti-fascists in the Market Place in May 1936 prior to a demonstration outside Granby Halls, where Mosley was speaking at a fascist rally.

The 1935 Peace Ballot

In 1935 the League of Nations Union initiated a public opinion poll on the subject of collective security. The Peace Ballot, as it became known, was carried out by volunteers and in Leicester over 2,000 canvassers worked for two months. Practically every street in the City was visited, with 50 organisations co-operating in the conduct of the ballot. 108,054 people voted, which was 66.2 per cent of the electorate. The results showed overwhelming support for the reduction of arms by international agreement, the prohibition of the manufacture and sale of arms for profit and for the use of sanctions (including military measures) against countries that attacked others. As a result of the ballot the Government was forced (briefly) to bring in sanctions against Italy for its invasion of Abyssinia.

PARLIAMENTARY ELECTION
SOUTH DIVISION

LESLIE MADDOCK
The Labour Candidate

R.T. Paget (above and below) addresses an election meeting in Whitwick during the 1935 General Election. Paget achieved some notoriety after being thrown out of Granby Halls by Mosley's blackshirts. Mosley even threatened to sue him in court over his interruptions. He later became an MP for Northampton.

PARLIAMENTARY ELECTION
WEST DIVISION

JOHN MORGAN
THE LABOUR CANDIDATE
Please hang this photo in your window

Above and below: Election material from Labour's unsuccessful candidates in the 1935 General Election.

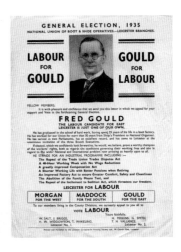

GENERAL ELECTION, 1935
NATIONAL UNION OF BOOT & SHOE OPERATIVES—LEICESTER BRANCHES.

LABOUR FOR **GOULD**   **GOULD** FOR **LABOUR**

FRED GOULD
THE LABOUR CANDIDATE FOR EAST
LEICESTER IS JUST ONE OF OUR OWN.

These banners were probably painted by local signwriter Harry Wright. Only Spinney Hill has survived boundary and ward name changes. The rising sun image of Socialism can be found on ILP graphics in the years before World War One. The Leicester Mercury *published the photograph of the North Braunstone Labour Party banner (bottom left) after it had been rediscovered in 1962. Like the other banners, it was probably painted some time after 1935, when the North Braunstone ward came into existence. Unfortunately, this banner has once again been lost.*

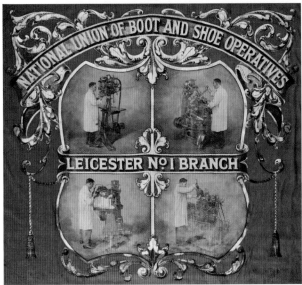

This double-sided banner served No.1 and No.2 branches of NUBSO. It is currently in store at Leicester Arts and Museum Service, awaiting a chance to be displayed. Bottom right: banner painters at work on the banner in 1935 at Tutills studio. Rose Thackery (left) specialised in painting the centres of banners, while Jack Pooley (working on the Leicester banner), was a signwriter. Tutills had been making regalia since the 1840s.

A Leicester Trades Council meeting, photographed by the British Council, c.1936. The man on his feet is Will Maw, a local teachers' leader. One delegate appears to be asleep.

Will Maw became president of the Trades Council in 1930 and was its general secretary from 1932–45. He came to Leicester in 1902 from Lincolnshire and became a delegate to the Trades Council from the National Federation of Class Teachers in 1909.

R.V. Walton (b.1894) was a Trades Council delegate from the Leatherworkers Union. Originally a member of the British Socialist Party, he then joined the Communist Party and was a local election candidate in 1932. He was active in the anti-fascist movement and by the mid-1930s he had left the CP. In 1937 he was elected president of the Leicester Co-operative Party.

Right: A Leicester Trades Council advert from 1930. During the 1930s trade union membership went into decline.

Some of the 50 Basque children at Evington Hall in July 1937.

Basque children at Evington Hall taking lessons in July 1937.

Basque Refugee Children come to Leicester

From July 1937, Leicester played host to 50 refugee Basque children. The 30 boys and 20 girls, aged between seven and 15, came from Bilbao, which was being bombed by the Fascists. The children arrived in Leicester from a camp in Southampton where 4,000 had arrived by boat. They were brought to Leicester by members of the Leicester Automobile Association and stayed at Evington Hall.

The British Government had only very reluctantly allowed them to come into the country and offered the refugees no support. In Leicester, local people helped through donations and voluntary subscription. Many of the children were 'adopted' by local people paying 10s a week. Twelve of the boys went to school in Leicester, while the others had classes in Spanish in Evington Hall. The secretary of the Leicester Committee for Basque children was Mary Attenborough, mother of Richard and David, and the matron was Spanish-speaking Miss McPhie.

Schoolteacher Dorothy Adams organised the children's shoe repairs at Wyggeston Girls School. Dorothy had taken lessons in cobbling at the technical college and then, with borrowed benches, knives and tools, had taught cobbling to sixth-form girls and her fellow teachers.

As Franco's military might conquered more territory, the pro-Fascist Committee for the Repatriation of Spanish Children, backed by the *Daily Mail*, campaigned to have the children sent back to Spain.

Basque refugee children peeling potatoes at Evington Hall.

Right: An advert for a Left Book Club meeting in 1938. The club rallied anti-fascists and the left against Chamberlain's appeasement of the Nazis.

Bert Bowden was elected to the city council in 1938 for the De Montfort ward. This election was the first step in a lengthy political career by one of Saffron Lane's most prominent citizens. 'Pilot officer' Bowden was elected as MP for Leicester South in 1945 and went on to fight and win six more elections. In 1964 he became Leader of the House of Commons and in 1966 was appointed Commonwealth Secretary.

Fred Watson was a conscientious objector during World War One and was sent to Dartmoor Prison. There were so many conscientious objectors in Dartmoor that an ILP branch was established in the prison. In 1927 he came to Leicester and became district secretary of the WEA and was still its honorary secretary in the 1970s. He was a member of the City Council for 13 years and was chairman of the Education Committee for five years.

In Conservative Evington it was probably thought a good idea to conceal the fact that Constance Brown was actually the Labour candidate.

The new Co-operative Hall and Education Centre at the corner of Belgrave Gate and Navigation Street, opened in November 1938. It was a converted church and had five classrooms and a hall seating 650 people.

Wagons of coal being uploaded at the Society's West Bridge Wharf for delivery to household by horse and cart, c.1939.

Cllr Sam Adams, the new president of the Leicester Co-operative Society, opens a shop on Bannerman Road in July 1936.

Local Volunteers for the International Brigade

Three Leicester men died fighting fascism during the Spanish Civil War. They were volunteers with the International Brigade. In February 1937, only months after his arrival, Fred Sykes was killed in the battle of Jamara. A 24-year-old shoe repairer, Jack Watson, was killed in December 1937 on the Pozoblanco front. Roy Watts, aged 24, was a

furniture salesman at the Leicester Co-op. He was killed in the battle of the Ebro in September 1938. Fred Sykes and Roy Watts were local Communist Party members.

Left: Roy Watts.

Right: Leicester Co-operative Magazine, *February 1938.*

KEEP ON SENDING MILK TO SPAIN!

A MILLION PEOPLE IN MADRID ARE SUFFERING THEIR SECOND WINTER OF WAR. MANY ARE SICK AND WOUNDED

Madrid's daily milk ration is only 1,000 gallons — for 1,000,000 people! Nobody over four years of age can get milk regularly.

All over democratic Spain food is scarce. **They Need Help Desperately.** More than anything else they need MILK.

Through the agency of the Co-operative Movement there is an easy way by which you can send the milk Spain needs so badly. Buy Sixpenny Tokens as often as you can! One large consignment of milk has already been sent to Spain by British sympathisers through this humanitarian scheme.

BUY SIXPENNY MILK FOR SPAIN TOKENS REGULARLY AT YOUR LOCAL L·C·S BRANCH

In January 1938 some of the refugees returned to Bilbao which was now in Franco's hands. The others stayed on in Leicester. Mary Attenborough argued that: 'if we were to write to the refugee mother of one of our families at Evington and say that we had decided to send her children back to Bilbao into the hands of those same people who are holding her husband prisoner, it would not be much comfort to her…It is difficult for her to realise that the same authority who is still bombing open towns and villages with unparalleled barbarity can be relied upon to treat her children with the "utmost kindness"…If we can send back children to parents with homes to receive them, then we think they should go, but we will never deliver up children to their parents' enemies'.

Local residents inspect the broken windows of the British Union of Fascists' HQ in Wellington Street in 1938. The night before, Oswald Mosley had held a meeting in the Corn Exchange.

Above: The LCS gas decontamination squad in 1939.

Above: Co-op Laundry workers coming out of their air-raid shelter in 1939.

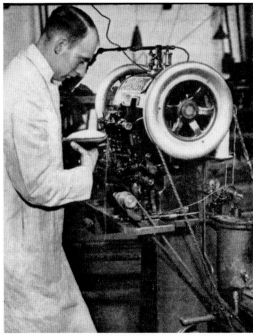

A machinist at work at the LCS Boot Repairing Factory, c.1939. When the Jarrow marchers arrived in Leicester in October 1936, their boots were falling to pieces. On their own initiative the Society's boot repairers sat up all night and worked without pay to repair the marchers' boots. One repairer remarked to Ellen Wilkinson MP, 'it seems sort of queer doing your own job just because you want to help, instead of doing it because you'd starve if you didn't'.

OVER 70,000 RESIDENTS enjoy the benefits of CO-OPERATIVE TRADING

NEARLY 1½ MILLIONS of the people's savings are safely held in trust and interest paid at an average rate of 3¼%

The Society contributes over £20,000 annually to the City Rates.

OVER 200,000 people are supplied with PURE FOODS each week

OVER £150,000 was paid out to members in dividend last year, contributing to the City's prosperity.

What Co-operation means to Leicester . . . .

It is inevitable that the largest retail distributive organisation in the City should have a profound influence upon the community. The Co-operative Society is more than a mere grocer's shop ; the facts reveal that it plays a vital part in the civic life.

Its prime function, however, is to supply reliable goods at reasonable prices, and its success can be measured by the annual turnover of £2,370,000.

Membership is Free and open to all

LEICESTER CO-OPERATIVE SOCIETY LIMITED

Registered Office : 4 UNION STREET
Telephone 20431

The Society provides employment for 2,000 persons under good conditions with an annual wage bill of nearly a Quarter of a million Pounds.

One of the LCS bread round men, c.1939. Sliced bread was not introduced until 1940.

Photographic Acknowledgments

Page

ii   The Record Office for Leicestershire, Leicester & Rutland.

iv   **A woman filling a bucket, White Street**, Ned Newitt.

vi   **Photos**, The Record Office for Leicestershire, Leicester & Rutland.

1   **Chartist handbill, 1848**, The Record Office for Leicestershire, Leicester & Rutland.

2   **Parliamentary election handbill**, 1837, B. Bilson.

3   **Framework Knitters**, Quilter J.H. & Chamberlain, J., *Framework Knitting and Hosiery Manufacture*, 1911; **Framework Knitters' petition**, The Record Office for Leicestershire, Leicester & Rutland.

4   **Chartist Handbill, 1848**, National Archives; **George Buckby**, The Record Office; **NCA Card**, Mark Crail.

5   **Handbill & William Holyoak**, The Record Office; **Josiah Gimson**, Gould, F.J., *A History Of The Leicester Secular Society*, Leicester 1900.

6   **Portrait of John Biggs**, unknown artist, Leicester Arts and Museum Service; **Michael Wright**, Gould, op. cit.

7   **Thomas Emery**, The Record Office for Leicestershire, Leicester & Rutland.

8–11   **Leicester Co-operative Society, engravings and photos**, *Co-operation in Leicester (Distributive Co-operation in Leicester)*, 1898 and Thompson, Stephen, J., *Social Redemption or The Fifty Years Story of the Leicester Co-operative Society Ltd 1860-1910*, Leicester 1911.

12–16   **Leicester Co-operative Hosiery Society**, Blandford, T. & Newell, G., *Leicester Co-operative Hosiery Manufacturing Society*, 1898.

17   **Framework Knitters**, Quilter J.H. & Chamberlain op. cit.; **Jimmy Holmes**, Leicester Trades Council, *Trade Union Congress Leicester, Official Souvenir*, 1903.

17   **Leicester Co-operative Hosiery Society**, Blandford, T. & Newell G., op. cit.

18–19   **Certificate and photos**, Richards, T.F. & Poulton E.L., *Fifty Years: Being The History Of The National Union Of Boot And Shoe Operatives*, Leicester Co-operative Printing Society, 1924.

20   **Secular Sunday School Band of Hope Pledge**, The Record Office; **Bertwal Cartoon**, *Leicester Pioneer*.

21   **Photos**, Biggs, J.T., *Sanitation versus Vaccination*, 1912.

22   **LCHS education room**, Blandford, T. & Newell G., op. cit.

23   **Old Stockingers**, *Illustrated London News*, 7 December 1889; **Edith Gittens**, Shirley Aucott; **Fanny Fullagar**, *Catalogue of the Leicester Commemoration Exhibition*, 1897.

24   **Causeway Lane Equity factory**, Greening, Edward O., *A Pioneer Co-partnership*, 1923.

25–26   **Interiors of Bede Street Equity factory**, Equity Shoes, Western Road, Leicester.

27   **William Morris handbill**, Special Collections of the Library of the University of Leicester; **Sunday Free Lecture poster, Secular Hall interior**, The Record Office.

28   **Tom Barclay**, Record Office; **Handbill and poster**, Special Collections of the Library of the University of Leicester.

29   **Burley's Yard and Abbey Street**, Ned Newitt.

30–32   **Handbills and poster**, Special Collections of the Library of the University of Leicester; **Archibald Gorrie**, Ned Newitt (copy of original lost from the Leicester Labour Archive).

33–35   **Handbills**, The Archive of The Independent Labour Party, London School of Economics; **Photos**, Leicester Trades Council, *Trade Union Congress Leicester 1903, Official Souvenir*, 1903.

36–37   **Amos Mann and adverts**, *A Souvenir of the 47th Co-operative Congress*, Manchester 1915; **Anchor Shoes**, Mann, A., *Democracy in Industry, A History of Anchor Shoes*, 1914.

36 & 41   **Handbills**, Special Collections of the Library of the University of Leicester.

38–39   **Cartoons**, *The Wyvern*; **Photos**, Richards, T.F. & Poulton E.L., op. cit.

40   **Photo**, The Record Office.

42–43   **Builders' Labourers Banner**, Leicester Arts and Museum Service; **Thurmaston Friendly Society Banner**, Thurmaston Heritage group, (photos Ned Newitt).

44   **Winifred Street flats, Taylor Street closets**, The Record Office.

45–46   **Great Central Railway Photos**, The Record Office.

48–49   **Photos**, Co-operation in Leicester and Member Relations Dept, Midland Co-operative Society.

50   **ILP Photo**, Maggie Ash; **Secular outing and election address**, Record Office; **Anti-Conscription pamphlet**, Special Collections of the Library of the University of Leicester.

51–53   **Photos**, The Labour Party Conference 1911, *Official Souvenir*, Leicester 1911, Leicester Trades Council, *Trade Union Congress Leicester 1903*.

54–5   **Photos**, *Leicester: A Souvenir of the 47th Co-operative Congress*, Manchester 1915, *Co-operation in Leicester*, op. cit.

56   **Photos and logos**, *Co-operation in Leicester*, op. cit.

57   **Frederick Sutton**, The Labour Party Conference, op. cit.

58   **Photos**, Leicester Co-operative Printing Society, *21 Years of Co-partnership Printing*, 1913.

59   **Barwell Co-op Boot and Shoe Manufacturing Society**, The Record Office.

60–67   **1905 March**, The Record Office.

68–69   **Photos**, *Leicester: A Souvenir of the 47th Co-operative Congress*, op. cit.; **Anchor Builders Photo**, *Leicester Mercury*.

70   **Photo of J.R. MacDonald**, Mrs J. Setchfield; **Bertwal Cartoon**, *Leicester Pioneer*.

71   **Election address**, The Archive of The Independent Labour Party.

72–73   **Cartoons**, Leicester Pioneer; **Photo**, The Labour Party Conference 1911, *Official Souvenir*, Leicester 1911.

74   **Annie Stretton**, Mrs J. Setchfield; **Mrs C. Wilson**, *Co-operative Magazine*.

75   **Co-op Women's Guild**, *Leicester: A Souvenir of the 47th Co-operative Congress*, op. cit., **Co-op Laundry**, ibid.

76–77   **Skiving by Sylvia Pankhurst**, Leicester Arts and Museum Service; **Untitled Gouache by Sylvia Pankhurst**, R. Pankhurst.

78   **Postcard**, Mrs J. Setchfield; **St Mark's interior**, The Labour Party Conference 1911, *Official Souvenir*, Leicester 1911.

79   **St Mark's Church**, Malcolm Elliott.

80–81   **Photos**, The Labour Party Conference 1911, *Official Souvenir*, Leicester 1911; **1911 Labour Conference**, The Record Office.

82   **Mrs Bell-Richards and handbill**, The Record Office; **T.F. Richards**, Trades Council Handbook, 1928.

83   **1911 Rail Strike**, The Record Office.

84   **John Murby**, The Record Office.

85   **Handbill**, The Record Office.

86–90   **Suffragettes**, The Record Office; **Equity Float**, Equity Shoes.

91   **Handbills and press photos**, Mrs J. Setchfield.

92–93   **Photos**, Beazley, Ben, *Leicester During The Great War*, Derby, 1999.

94   **Photos**, The Record Office.

95   **Postcard and handbills**, Mrs J. Setchfield.

96–97   **Photos**, The Record Office; **Handbill**, Mrs J. Setchfield.

98   **Russell's factory**, The Record Office; **John Pantling**, Martin Pantling; **Jabez Chaplin**, Howes, C. (ed), *Leicester: Its Civic, Industrial, Institutional and Social Life*, Leicester 1927.

99   **Handbill and election address**, Mrs J. Setchfield; **Photo**, The Record Office.

100   **Photos**, *Leicester Mercury and Leicester Pioneer*.

101   **Amos Sherriff**, The Record Office.

101   **Co-op Tailoring Dept**, The Record Office; **Photos**, *Leicester Pioneer*.

102   **Unidentified Co-op Store**, Member Relations Dept, Midland Co-operative Society; **Central Butchery Store**, *Leicester Co-operative Magazine* 1923.

104   **Election address**, The Archive of The Independent Labour Party, London School of Economics; **Photo of Banton and Howard**, Ned Newitt (copy of original lost from the Leicester Labour Archive).

105   **Alf Hill**, Trades Council Handbooks; **Emily Fortey**, Howes, C. (ed), op. cit.; **1925 election address**, Leicester Labour Archive.

106   **Photos**, *Leicester Co-operative Magazine*, 1923.

107–08   **Wigston Hosiers photos**, Greening, Edward O., *A Democratic Co-partnership*, Leicester, 1921.

109 & 111   **Photos**, *Leicester Co-operative Magazine*, 1923–29.

110   **Leicester Carriage Builders and Wheelwrights**, *Leicester Carriage Builders* and *Leicester Co-operative Magazine*, 1923.

112   **Labour gala**, Ned Newitt (copy of lost original); **Pethick-Lawrence poster**, Leicester Labour Archive; **Election result**, Howard, W., *Fifty Years of Progress The History of the Labour Party in Leicester, 1903-1950*, Leicester, 1950.

113   **Gooding Avenue**, Housing Dept, Leicester City Council; **Hallam and Housing Committee**, Howes op cit.

114   **Park Estate being built**, The Record Office; **Boot houses on the Park estate**, Housing Dept, Leicester City Council.

115   **Braunstone council houses**, Housing Dept, Leicester City Council.

116   **Photos and advert**, *Leicester Co-operative Magazine* 1923–26.

117   **General strike photos**, *Leicester Mercury* and *Leicester Evening Mail*.

118–19   **NUBSO certificate**, Richards, T.F. & Poulton E.L., op. cit.; **Mrs Bell-Richards**, Ned Newitt; **E.L. Poulton**, Howes op. cit.; Parbury, Adnitt & Baum, Trades Council Yearbooks; **NUBSO memorial**, Richards, T.F. & Poulton E.L., op. cit.

120–21   **Photos**, Howes op. cit.; **T.R. Hill**, Mrs J. Setchfield; **Sam Cooper**, Ned Newitt (copy of lost original).

121   **Conservative Cartoons**, Leicester Labour Archive; **Photos**, Howes op. cit.

122   **Cartoon**, Leicester Labour Archive; **The Council Chamber**, The Record Office.

123   **Leicester Labour gala photos**, Ned Newitt (copies of originals lost from the Labour archive).

124   **1929 election address**, Leicester Labour Archive; **Wilton Street**, *Leicester Mercury*; **Harrison and Hayes**, The Record Office.

125–26   **Photos**, *Leicester Co-op Magazine* 1929.

127   **Gypsy Lane Co-op Laundry**, Member Relations Dept, Midland Co-operative Society.

128   **Cartoon and handbill**, Leicester Labour Archive; **Photos**, *Leicester Mercury*.

129,   **Photos**, *Leicester Mercury* and *Leicester Evening Mail*.

130   **Wolsey strikers leaving the Corn Exchange**, The Record Office.

131–33   **Photos**, *Leicester Mercury* and *Leicester Evening Mail*; T. F. Richards, Trades Council yearbook, 1928.

134–37   **Leicester slums**, Ned Newitt.

139   **Penny Bank Gala**, *Leicestershire Co-op Magazine*.

140   **Humberstone Road Co-op**, Member Relations Dept, Midland Co-operative Society.

141   **High Street Co-op**, *Leicester Co-op Magazine*.

142   **Photos**, *Leicester Mercury* and *Leicester Evening Mail*.

143   **Photos**, Ned Newitt (copy of lost original); **Election addresses**, Leicester Labour Archive.

144   **Labour Party banners**, Leicester South Labour Party, (photos Ned Newitt).

145   **NUBSO Banner**, Leicester Arts and Museum Service (photo Ned Newitt); **NUBSO banner being painted**, Gorman, John, *Banner Bright*, London, 1973; **Lost Labour banner**, *Leicester Mercury*.

146   **Trades Council photos**, The Record Office; **Trades Council advert**, Leicester Labour Archive.

147   **Photos**, *Leicester Mercury* and *Leicester Co-op Magazine*.

148   **Photos and adverts**, *Leicester Co-op Magazine*; **Calling cards**, Leicester Labour Archive.

149   **Photos and adverts**, *Leicester Co-op Magazine*, 1936–38.

150   **Photos**, *Leicester Mercury* and *Leicester Co-op Magazine*, 1938.

151   **Photos**, *Leicester Co-op Magazine*, 1939.

Bibliography

Archives and Primary Sources
Leicester Arts and Museum Service.
The Leicester Labour Archive.
The Archive of the Independent Labour Party, London School of Economics.
The Author's Collection.
The *Leicester Mercury*.
The Leicestershire Record Office.
The Midlands Co-operative Society, Member Relations, Leicester.
The National Archive.
The Papers of T. Rowland Hill (Mrs J. Setchfield).
The Special Collections of the Library of the University of Leicester.

Books and Pamphlets
Aucott, Shirley, *Mothercraft and Maternity*, Leicester, 1997.
Barclay, Tom, *Memoirs and Medleys, The Autobiography of a Bottle Washer*, 1934.
Beazley, Ben, *Leicester During The Great War*, Derby, 1999.
Bellamy, J.M. and J. Saville, (eds), *The Dictionary of Labour Biography* (11 vols).
Biggs, J.T., *Sanitation versus Vaccination*, 1912.
Blandford, T. & G. Newell, *Leicester Co-operative Hosiery Manufacturing Society*, 1898.
Fox, Alan, *A History of the National Union of Boot and Shoe Workers*, 1958.
Gorman, John, *Banner Bright*, London, 1973.
——— *To Build Jerusalem*, London, 1980.
Gould, F.J., *A History of The Leicester Secular Society*, Leicester, 1900.
Greening, Edward O., *A Pioneer Co-partnership*, 1923.
——— *A Democratic Co-partnership*, Leicester, 1921.
Gurnham, Richard, *The Hosiery Unions 1776–1976*, 1976.
Howard, W., *Fifty Years of Progress The History of the Labour Party in Leicester, 1903–1950*, Leicester, 1950.
Howes, C. (ed.), *Leicester: Its Civic, Industrial, Institutional and Social Life*, Leicester, 1927.
Jenkins, Jess, *Leicester's 1905 Unemployment March*, Leicester, 2006.
Jenkins, Robin, *Leicestershire People*, 1996.
Lancaster, Bill, *Radicalism Cooperation and Socialism: Leicester Working Class Politics 1860–1906*, Leicester, 1987.
Leicester Co-operative Printing Society, *21 Years of Co-partnership Printing*, 1913.
Leicester Co-operative Society, *Co-operation in Leicester* (Distributive Co-operation in Leicester), 1898.
Leicester Trades Council, *Trade Union Congress Leicester 1903*, Official Souvenir, 1903.
Leicester: A Souvenir of the 47th Co-operative Congress, Manchester, 1915.
Mann, Amos, *Democracy In industry, A History of Anchor Shoes*, 1914.
Merrick, Daniel, *The Warp of Life*, Leicester, 1876.
Nash, David & David Reeder (eds), *Leicester in the Twentieth Century*, Leicester, 1993.
Nash, David, *Secularism, Art and Freedom*, Leicester, 1992.
Pankhurst, Richard, *Sylvia Pankhurst Artist and Crusader*, London, 1979.
Plumb, J.H., *A History of Leicester Co-operative Boot and Shoe Society*, 1936.
Quilter J.H. & J. Chamberlain, *Framework Knitting and Hosiery Manufacture*, 1911.
Richards, T.F. & E.L. Poulton, *Fifty Years: Being The History Of The National Union Of Boot And Shoe Operatives*, 1924.
Roberts, Stephen, and Dorothy Thompson (eds), *Images of Chartism*, 1998.
Thompson, Stephen J., *Social Redemption or The Fifty Years Story of the Leicester Co-operative Society Ltd 1860–1910*, Leicester, 1911.
The Labour Party Conference 1911, Official Souvenir, Leicester, 1911.
Whitmore, Dr Richard, *Alice Hawkins and the Suffragette Movement in Edwardian Leicester*, Derby, 2007.

Newspapers and Periodicals
Leicester Chronicle.
Leicester Evening Post.
Leicester Mercury.
The Leicester Pioneer.
Leicester Co-operative Magazine.
Leicester Co-operative Record.
The Chartist Pilot.
The Leicestershire Movement.
The Midland Counties Illuminator.
The South Midlands Free Press.
The Wyvern.